CARIBBEAN SEA

ATLANTIC OCEAN

PUNTA DE GALLINAS

Gulf of Honduras

INDIES

GUADELOUPE (Fr.)

MARTINIQUE (Fr.)

BARBADOS

TRINIDAD AND TOBAGO

Port of Spain

Barranquilla
Cartagena
Panamá
IST. OF PAN.
Golfo de

Maracaibo
Valencia
CARACAS
La Guaira
Mérida
Ciudad Bolívar
Cerro Icutú 7800
Georgetown
Paramaribo
Cayenne

VENEZUELA
GUYANA
SURINAME
FR. GUIANA

Medellín
BOGOTÁ
COLOMBIA
Boa Vista do Rio Branco
GUIANA HIGHLANDS

ISLA DE MALPELO (Colombia)

Nevado del Tolima 17 110

ISLA DE COCO (Costa Rica)

ERICA
ICARAGUA

Quito
Cotopaxi 19 347
Chimborazo 20 561
ECUADOR
Guayaquil

ARCHIPIÉLAGO DE COLÓN (GALÁPAGOS ISLANDS) (Ec.)

Golfo de Guayaquil

Iquitos
Leticia

Manaus (Manáos)

Río Negro
Río Solimões (Amazonas)
Río Amazonas
Japurá
Putumayo

Equator

ILHA DE MARAJÓ

Belém (Pará)
São Luís (Maranhão)

ROCEDOS SÃO PEDRO E SÃO PAULO (Brazil)

Chiclayo
Trujillo
Nevs. Huascarán 22 205

PERU
LIMA
Callao
Cuzco
Arequipa
Volcán Misti 19 098
Mollendo

Juruá
Purus
Río Madeira
Río Branco
Pôrto Velho
Xingu
Tocantins

B R A Z I L
CHAPADA DE MATO GROSSO
Cuiabá
Brasília
Diamantino
Belo Horizonte
Pco. do Bandeira 9482

Fortaleza (Ceará)
Teresina
Natal
João Pessoa (Paraíba)
RECIFE (Pernambuco)
Maceió
Salvador (Bahia)

ARQUIPÉLAGO FERNANDO DE NORONHA (Brazil)

CABO DE SÃO ROQUE

SERRA DO PIAUÍ
BRAZILIAN HIGHLANDS
SERRA DO ESPINHAÇO

Antofagasta
ISLA DE SAN FÉLIX (Chile)
ISLA DE SAN AMBROSIO (Chile)
Copiapó
Coquimbo
Valparaíso
SANTIAGO
ISLAS DE JUAN FERNÁNDEZ (Chile)

La Paz
Nev. Illimani 21 201
Sucre
Potosí
BOLIVIA
GRAN CHACO
PARAGUAY
Asunción
Cerro Azufre (Copiapó) 6442
Salta
Tucumán
Córdoba
Cerro 22 880
Mendoza
Rosario
Santa Fe

Iquique

Tropic of Capricorn

SÃO PAULO
Santos
RIO DE JANEIRO
CABO FRIO
Vitória
Florianópolis
Pôrto Alegre
Río Grande

ATLANTIC OCEAN

Corrientes
Salto
URUGUAY
MONTEVIDEO
BUENOS AIRES
La Plata
Río de la Plata
PAMPAS
Bahía Blanca
Concepción
Valdivia
Puerto Montt
ISLA DE CHILOÉ

A R G E N T I N A
C H I L E
ANDES MTS.

PACIFIC OCEAN

Viedma
Golfo San Matías

ARCHIPIÉLAGO DE LOS CHONOS
Monte San Valentín 13 314
Comodoro Rivadavia
Golfo San Jorge

FALKLAND IS. (ISLAS MALVINAS) (Br.)
Río Gallegos
Stanley

WELLINGTON
HANOVER
Punta Arenas
DESOLACIÓN
Mt. Sarmiento 8100
TIERRA DEL FUEGO
ISLA DE LOS ESTADOS
CABO DE HORNOS (CAPE HORN)
Estrecho de Magallanes

SOUTH GEORGIA (Falkland Is.)

Drake Passage

SOUTH SANDWICH ISLANDS (Falkland Is.)

SOUTH ORKNEY IS. (B.A.T.)

SOUTH SHETLAND ISLANDS (B.A.T.)

JOINVILLE

ANTARCTIC PENINSULA

JAMES ROSS

Antarctic Circle

Longitude West of Greenwich

Relief		
Meters		Feet
3050		10 000
1525		5000
610		2000
305		1000
0	Sea Level	0
152.5		500
1525		5000
3050		10 000
6100		20 000

110° 100° 90° 80° 70° 60° 50° 40° 30° 20° 10°

10° 0° 10° 20° 30° 40° 50° 60°

Enchantment of the World

VENEZUELA

By Marion Morrison

Consultant for Venezuela: George I. Blanksten, Ph.D., Professor Emeritus of Political Science, Northwestern University, Evanston, Illinois

Consultant for Reading: Robert L. Hillerich, Ph.D., Bowling Green State University, Bowling Green, Ohio

CP CHILDRENS PRESS®
CHICAGO

A young girl wears a festive hat for the yearly carnival in Caracas.

Picture Acknowledgments
© **Photri, Inc.:** 4, 43, 61 (right), 90 (right)
© **Chip & Rosa Maria Peterson:** 5, 6, 10, 14 (left), 37 (right), 66 (bottom left & right), 69 (left), 71 (left), 74 (left), 79, 82 (2 photos), 83 (right)
Shostal, Inc.: 8, 12 (left), 16 (bottom left), 21, 31 (right), 32 (top right & bottom), 35, 68 (left), 77 (left), 83 (left), 97, 112; © Hubertus Kanus: cover, 16 (bottom right), 62 (left), 63 (2 photos), 72, 78 (bottom); © Manley Photo-Tuscon, Ariz.: 22, 24 (right); © Dr. Nigel Smith: 30 (right); © Leonard Lee Rue: 32 (top left); © Eric G. Carle: 102
© **Tony Morrison, South America Pictures:** 11, 14 (right), 15 (left), 16 (top), 18 (right), 24 (left), 28, 29 (right), 31 (left), 37 (left), 40 (left), 58 (2 photos), 59, 61 (left), 65 (left), 66 (top), 68 (right), 78 (top), 80 (top left & top right), 85, 86 (2 photos), 87, 113 (right)
© **Superstock International, Inc.:** 12 (right)
© **Cameramann Int., Ltd.:** 13 (2 photos), 18 (left), 27, 49, 69 (right), 71 (right), 74 (right), 76 (2 photos), 77 (right), 80 (bottom left & right), 90 (left), 92, 95, 99, 100, 101, 105 (2 photos), 106, 113 (left)
Root Resources: © Jane P. Downton: 15 (right); © Hans Hasen: 29 (left), 40 (right); © Irene Hubbell: 110
© **Victor Englebert:** 20, 30 (top & bottom left), 62 (right), 64 (2 photos), 65 (right)
Historical Pictures Service, Chicago: 45, 48, 50, 51 (2 photos), 54
Len W. Meents: Maps on pages 11, 13, 16, 21, 22, 55
Courtesy Flag Research Center, Winchester, Massachusetts 01890: Flag on back cover
Cover: Beach and marina at Puerto la Cruz

Library of Congress Cataloging-in-Publication Data

Morrison, Marion.
  Venezuela / by Marion Morrison.
    p.   cm. — (Enchantment of the world)
  Includes index.
  Summary: Discusses the history, geography, people, and culture of the country called "Little Venice" by the first Spanish explorers.
  ISBN 0-516-02711-5
  1. Venezuela—Juvenile
literature. [1. Venezuela.] I. Title. II. Series.
F2308.5.M673 1989   88-30493
987—dc19   CIP
                                   AC

A woman wears a straw hat to protect her from the sun.

TABLE OF CONTENTS

A lush valley in the Andes

Chapter 1

A VARIED LAND

The Republic of Venezuela is in the north of South America. It has a coastline on the Caribbean Sea and its northeast shore faces the Atlantic Ocean. East of Venezuela is the Republic of Guyana; to the south, Brazil; and to the south and southwest, Colombia. With a total of 352,145 square miles (912,050 square kilometers), Venezuela is similar in size to the combined states of Texas and Kansas in the United States or four times the size of Great Britain. It is the sixth largest country in South America.

Venezuela lies just to the north of the equator and almost half the country is covered by some form of forest. Elsewhere the land is varied. Venezuela has snowcapped mountains, plains, and grasslands, one of South America's greatest rivers, the Orinoco, some desert, and many superb beaches.

When Spanish explorers first arrived on the north coast of Venezuela at the beginning of the sixteenth century, they noted native Indian huts built on stilts in the coastal lakes and rivers. The scene reminded them of Venice and so they named the country "Little Venice," or Venezuela.

In Venezuela there was no great empire like the Incas of Peru or the Aztecs of Mexico, and no obvious mineral wealth like the

An aerial view of the Andes

silver mines of Potosí in Bolivia. So there was no great rush to
colonize the territory and it was many years before the country
was fully explored.

Venezuela declared its independence from Spain in 1811 and
this was finally secured in 1830. The new Republic of Venezuela
remained a relatively poor, agricultural country until the early
twentieth century. The turning point in Venezuela's fortunes
occurred in 1922 when huge deposits of oil were confirmed in the
region of Lake Maracaibo. This tarry substance, once used by
Indians to waterproof their boats, transformed the economy and
brought the country great wealth.

Chapter 2

VENEZUELA: LAND
OF EL DORADO

The great variety of physical features in Venezuela accounts for the different ways of life of the people, and the different climate experienced in each region. There are six distinct regions. The first two are the Andes mountains in the west and the coastal highlands in the north. Between these two ranges, and making the third region, are the lower Segovia highlands. The fourth region is the coast; the fifth is the Llanos, or grasslands, in the center of the country; and sixth is Guiana in the south. Sometimes considered as another, separate region is the Maracaibo Basin that lies between two branches of the Andes mountains in the northwest.

THE ANDES

The magnificent Andes mountains run for 4,500 miles (7,242 kilometers) from the southern tip of South America to the Caribbean coast in the north. On the border of Colombia and Venezuela the chain divides. One range, the Sierra de Perijá continues north, forming part of the frontier between the two countries. It then tapers off into the Guajira Peninsula west of the

Pico Bolívar bathed in the rays of the setting sun

Gulf of Venezuela. The other range is called the Sierra Nevada de Mérida and it extends in a northeasterly direction across Venezuela to the Caribbean Sea. Venezuela's highest mountain, the Pico Bolívar at 16,423 feet (5,002 meters) is in the Sierra Nevada de Mérida. Several of the peaks in this range are permanently snow covered. This part of the country is often referred to locally as the "roof of Venezuela."

Traditionally these mountains are the home of Andean Indians, and a few communities still tend their cows and sheep on the high slopes. But it is a harsh life as the soil is poor, and the extreme temperatures of the daytime sun and the cold at night make cultivation difficult.

Most people prefer to live below 5,000 feet (1,524 meters) in green, fertile valleys where they can grow maize (corn) and other crops. The valleys are fed by many streams that flow down the mountainsides from the snows above.

Fertile areas
of the
Sierra Nevada
de Mérida

The main towns are at this level, including Trujillo, Valera, San Cristóbal, and Mérida, founded in 1558. Mérida lies on a small tableland, or mesa, overlooked by the Pico Bolívar. The world's highest cable car runs between Mérida and Pico Espejo at 15,634 feet (4,765 meters). From this point, often deep in snow, there is a magnificent panorama of the surrounding mountains and valleys.

THE COASTAL HIGHLANDS

The coastal highlands is the most important region in Venezuela. They cover only 3 percent of the country, but the

*Caracas (above) lies at the base
of Avila mountain (left)*

majority of people live there. No peak is more than 10,000-feet
(3,048-meters) high, and in many places, particularly in the east,
dense forest covers the mountain slopes.

Three of Venezuela's most important towns are in fertile valleys
in this region. Caracas, the capital, lies at the foot of Avila
mountain. It is 3,150 feet (960 meters) above sea level and has a
temperate climate all year round. For many years Caracas was just
a small colonial settlement, until, with the wealth derived from
oil, it was transformed into one of the most sophisticated, modern
cities of the South American continent.

About 62 miles (100 kilometers) to the west of Caracas, and
1,476 feet (450 meters) above sea level is Lake Valencia, and the
nearby towns of Maracay and Valencia. This basin is the most
important agricultural and industrial area in the country. A
variety of factories line the shore of the freshwater lake, filling the

A pool with fountains (above) decorates the twin towers of Simón Bolívar complex. A panoramic view of Caracas (left)

sky with billowing smoke. Between the factories, people work hard cultivating fields of sugarcane and vegetables, against a noisy background of constant traffic moving between Caracas and Valencia.

THE SEGOVIA HIGHLANDS

The Segovia highlands, in the northwest, is a region of low hills and plains, nowhere more than 2,600 feet (792 meters) high and covered in dry, thorny scrub. Despite the arid climate, it is a productive agricultural region. Since colonial times there have been sugar and cocoa plantations and the land is particularly suitable for rearing goats. Venezuela's first copper mines were discovered here in 1605, and the importance of the zone as a mining region led to the construction of the country's first railway

13

*The sprawling city of Barquisimeto (left) and sugarcane
fields (right) near the coastal highlands*

line to take the minerals from the highlands to the coast. South of
the Segovia highlands is Barquisimeto, founded as a mining
settlement, and now Venezuela's fourth-largest city.

THE COAST

The Venezuelan coastline is made up of many different
geographical features. In the extreme east, in the part of the coast
facing the Atlantic Ocean, lies the territory of the Amacuro Delta.
This is the delta of the Orinoco River and it occupies about 250
miles (402 kilometers) of the coast. Many famous explorers made
their way into the South American hinterland through this
swampy delta.

Between the Paria Peninsula in the east and the Paraguaná
Peninsula in the west, Venezuela's Caribbean coastline can be
roughly divided by the Unare River Basin into two sections. The

A palm-shaded beach near Puerto la Cruz (left) and the harbor at Margarita Island (right)

Paria Peninsula is dry, with an important salt deposit that has been worked for many centuries.

The remainder of this part of the coast has many beautiful palm-fringed beaches and small fishing villages. Behind the beaches, forested highlands form a steep barrier the early explorers found difficult to cross, so many early Spanish settlements were located in the narrow coastal strip. Cumaná at the mouth of the Manzanares River was founded in 1520 and is the oldest Spanish town in South America. With neighboring Barcelona, it was a center for the pearl trade of the nearby islands of Cubagua and Margarita.

Venezuela owns some islands off the Caribbean coast, and Margarita, sometimes called "The Pearl of Venezuela," is the largest. Most of the population live in the developed eastern part and many tourists enjoy the picturesque beaches and seas, which

Above: The sand dunes of Coro
Below: Colorful old buildings (left) and the
modern business area (right) of Maracaibo

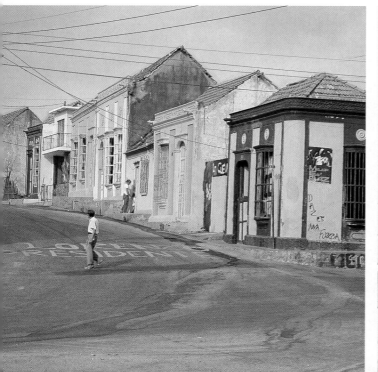

are good for surfing. The western part of the island is hotter and more barren and inhabited mainly by goats and deer.

Although this stretch of the coast is well developed for tourism, there is also a great deal of commercial activity. Much of it is centered in Puerto la Cruz, once a small fishing village and now the world's fifth oil shipping port. Venezuela's most important coal mines are also in this region, at Naricual just a few miles south of Barcelona. However the country's two main ports are located on the Caribbean coast to the west of the Unare Basin. They are La Guaira and Puerto Cabello.

This part of the coast is rocky in places and covered in dry scrub and cactus where the mountains descend close to the sea. There are also some very fine beaches, such as Choroní and Cata, which were trading harbors for cocoa and coffee in colonial days.

An extraordinary feature farther west along the coast are the sand dunes of Coro. Coro, an attractive old, historic city, stands on the mainland end of an isthmus leading to the peninsula of Paraguaná. The peninsula and the isthmus are flanked by broad sandy beaches swept by winds from the east. Along the isthmus the sand is constantly moving because large dunes and even the sparse vegetation typical of the region do not take hold. For a few miles along the isthmus, the aspect is pure desert and the road from Coro to the peninsula has to be kept clear by constant scraping and maintenance. So unique in Venezuela is this region that it has been decreed a national park.

THE MARACAIBO BASIN

Lake Maracaibo lies between the Sierra de Perijá and the Cordillera de Mérida in the northwest corner of Venezuela. With

Oil derricks (left) in Lake Maracaibo and the Rafael Urdaneta Bridge (right), the longest prestressed concrete span in the world

a surface area of about 5,000 square miles (12,950 square kilometers), it is the largest lake in South America.

Spanning the lake from east to west, is the Rafael Urdaneta Bridge, constructed in 1963. It is an impressive piece of engineering 5 miles (8 kilometers) long and 164 feet (50 meters) above sea level, with the longest prestressed concrete span in the world. The bridge is just one result of the development the discovery of oil has brought to the region.

The lake itself is covered by a forest of oil derricks. And where once small colonial settlements of stilted houses stood on the shore of the lake, there are now industrial oil towns like Ciudad Ojeda and Cabimas, and the capital of the region, Maracaibo.

Before the discovery of oil, the people of Maracaibo earned money transporting coffee from the mountains to the coast. The city still has the feel of a frontier town, even though in the last sixty years it has grown to more than five times its original size.

Some of the old buildings have been retained, particularly around the docks where small adobe houses line the narrow streets.

The Maracaibo Basin is excessively hot and humid. There is very little wind and the rainfall is one of the highest in South America.

THE LLANOS

The Llanos is the name given to the immense central grassland plains that cover approximately one-third of Venezuela. To the north and west they are bordered by the Andes mountains, and to the east and south by the Orinoco River and the Guiana highlands.

Most of the Llanos lie at about 100 feet (30 meters) above sea level, but close to the Andean foothills they are higher. Where the Llanos are at their lowest, in the center of the grassland, there is annual flooding from the numerous, slow-running rivers that cross the region.

The land and the climate are harsh. Stretching out to the horizon in every direction, the flat expanse of grass is broken by only a few scattered trees. There is no shelter from the scorching midday sun and the frequent heavy rains. Severe droughts can occur between January and April, and the worst of the rains are from June to October.

Alexander von Humboldt, the scientist and naturalist, explored the Llanos early in the year 1800. It was a depressing experience. He wrote, "All around us the plains seemed to reach to the sky, and this vast and profound solitude looked like an ocean covered with seaweed."

In von Humboldt's day, as now, millions of cattle are raised in

Venezuelan cowboys rounding up cattle on the Llanos

the Llanos. The naturalist found that the only inhabitants able to withstand the hostile conditions were a few hardy missionaries and the cattlemen responsible for the great herds. And even today, only 13 percent of the population lives in this extensive area.

The twentieth century brought changes, however, with the construction of roads and the discovery of oil in east and central Llanos. Towns like Barinas and El Tigre have developed. The need to cultivate more crops to feed the growing towns has resulted in projects like the Guárico Dam near Calabozo. By controlling floodwater for use during droughts, dams are helping convert parts of the Llanos into fertile land.

GUIANA HIGHLANDS

The Guiana highlands and the Federal Territory of Amazonas in the south cover about half of Venezuela. The region is a jungle of

Tepuis *loom in the distance of the Guiana highlands.*

forested hills, rich grasslands, narrow valleys, swift-running rivers, and high granite tablelands that loom above the surrounding forest.

The tablelands are called *tepuis* and are part of the Guiana Shield, a rock formation considered to be one of the oldest in the world. This is the legendary land of Arthur Conan Doyle's *Lost World* filled with prehistoric animals. It was also the "golden world," and *El Dorado*, of explorers like Sir Francis Drake. Today, it is the real world of communities of forest Indians whose lives have changed very little for hundreds of years.

Some of the tepuis are as high as 6,000 feet (1,829 meters) and the most famous is Auyán-Tepui at 8,400 feet (2,560 meters), in a region to the southeast of the highlands, called *La Gran Sabana*, or the Great Plain. It owes its fame in part to Jimmy Angel, an American pilot, who in 1935 was the first to see the world's highest waterfall from the cockpit of his single-engined plane.

21

The Angel Falls cascade down the side of Auyán-Tepui.

The Angel Falls cascade some 3,212 feet (979 meters) down the side of Auyán-Tepui, creating great clouds of mist as they reach the bottom. They are sixteen times the height of Niagara Falls.

The region of Guiana has been developing rapidly because of its mineral resources and its economic and industrial potential. The historic colonial town of Ciudad Bolívar on the Orinoco River is at the center of this development, and nearby a new industrial complex based at Puerto Ordaz is being created.

THE ORINOCO RIVER

The most important river in Venezuela is the Orinoco. After the Amazon and the Plate River system in the southern half of the continent, the Orinoco is the third-largest in South America. The Magdalena River system in Colombia ranks fourth.

Orinoco is derived from the language of the Warao Indians who live in the delta, but different interpretations have been given as to its meaning. These include "father of our land" and "a place to paddle."

The river is 1,284 miles (2,066 kilometers) long and the Orinoco River Basin covers an area of 366,000 square miles (948,000 square kilometers). Seventy percent of the national territory, fifteen out of the twenty Venezuelan states, the Amazonas Territory, the greatest part of the Andes, and the Colombian Llanos empty their water either partly or solely into the Orinoco.

The source of the river was disputed for a long time, but in 1952, it was confirmed to be in the Guiana highlands, at about 3,500 feet (1,067 meters), near the Brazilian border.

Descending from these heights, the upper Orinoco is fast flowing with waterfalls and rapids. It then forms part of the frontier with neighboring Colombia, as it begins a long arclike course toward the mouth on the Atlantic coast. On its way it flows around the southern edge of the Llanos, where it is joined by many tributaries including the Apure River.

One of the largest tributaries in the Caroní River, which meets the Orinoco after plunging over the spectacular Caroní Falls not far from the delta.

A maze of small islands fill the delta surrounded by *canos*, or channels, through which the water forces its way into the ocean. Such is the force with which the water enters the Atlantic that there is fresh water several miles out to sea. The first European to reach the Orinoco and to notice this phenomenon was Christopher Columbus, in August 1498.

*The Orinoco River flows through a dense tropical rain
forest (left). Caroní Rapids in Canaima National Park (right)*

Large steamers can navigate upriver for about 700 miles (1,127
kilometers) and recent dredging has made it possible for
oceangoing vessels to make their way 226 miles (364 kilometers)
upriver. Seasonal rainfall from April to October can sometimes
increase the depth of the river as much as four times. In the
lowlands of the river basin, where there is annual flooding, some
places have been known to be 65 feet (20 meters) underwater.

The Orinoco is connected to the Amazon River system by the
Casiquiare Channel. This was first noted by Jesuit missionaries in
1744 and then confirmed by Alexander von Humboldt. The
connection occurs when some waters from the Upper Orinoco
break away and flow 220 miles (354 kilometers) south through
the Casiquiare into the Río Negro, a major Amazon tributary. It is
a wilderness part of the highlands, isolated, inhospitable, and
desolate, and it seems unlikely that the link between these two
great rivers will ever be put to good use.

SEASONS

Venezuela has a tropical climate and seasons are determined by rainfall rather than temperature. There are two seasons, known as the dry and rainy seasons. The dry season occurs from November through February or March, and the rainy season from April to October or November. The amount of rain depends on the region. For example, a minimal amount falls on parts of the coast, while in the Guiana highlands there is some rain all year round.

CLIMATIC ZONES

The temperature in most of the country depends on the altitude, wind, and proximity to the sea. Venezuela can be divided into six climatic zones.

The tropical, or hot zone, lies between sea level and 2,600 feet (792 meters). Maracaibo, at sea level, has an average annual temperature of 82 degrees Fahrenheit (27.8 degrees Celsius). To the south of Lake Maracaibo a strange phenomenon occurs, which has given the Catacumbo River the local name of the ''Lighthouse of Maracaibo.'' Due to a particular converging of winds, the almost nightly torrential cloudburst is accompanied by extraordinary lightning.

The subtropical zone stretches from 2,600 feet (792 meters) to about 5,000 feet (1,524 meters). Caracas is in this zone and has a reputation for its fine climate. As the Venezuelan writer, Oviedo y Baños, wrote: ''Caracas . . . seems to have been chosen by spring for its permanent home . . . '' The temperature changes little, ranging only between 64 and 72 degrees Fahrenheit (17.8 and 22.2 degrees Celsius) throughout the year.

From 5,000 to 7,250 feet (1,524 to 2,210 meters) is the temperate zone. Mérida in the Andes at 5,380 feet (1,640 meters) is in this zone and the mean temperature of the city is 66.2 degrees Fahrenheit (19 degrees Celsius).

The cold zone is 7,250 to about 10,000 feet (2,210 to 3,048 meters). Mucuchies, at just under 9,777 feet (2,980 meters) in the Andes, has recorded the lowest average temperature in Venezuela for an inhabited place of 52 degrees Fahrenheit (11 degrees Celsius).

The *páramo* zone lies from 10,000 to 15,000 feet (3,048 to 4,572 meters) and the perpetually cold zone is above that level.

NATURAL RESOURCES

Early explorers were disappointed not to find El Dorado, the land of gold and silver, in Venezuela. It is only in the twentieth century that prospectors began to discover how rich the republic really is in resources.

The largest deposits of oil are in the Maracaibo Basin, but others have been located in the Llanos and north of the Orinoco River.

As a second power resource, there is great potential for hydroelectricity in the country's fast-flowing rivers. A variety of minerals, including iron, gold, diamonds, copper, and bauxite are known to exist in Guiana. Exploitation of these resources is at an early stage.

The extensive grasslands of the Llanos continue to provide grazing for millions of cattle, and there is a varied catch in saltwater and freshwater fish. Within the immense forests of Venezuela there is plentiful timber.

Guri Dam, on the Caroní River, is one of the largest hydroelectric plants in the world.

POTENTIAL

Venezuela has great potential. For most of the twentieth century exploitation of oil brought the country great wealth. The recent collapse in world oil prices has changed the country's outlook. Now burdened with international foreign debts, Venezuela is looking to diversify its economy by exploiting its many other resources.

FLORA

In Venezuela there is an immense variety of trees and other plants. Different species are found in different habitats. On an Andean mountain slope their variety is clearly visible.

Immediately below the snow line, the slopes are covered with mountain vegetation of tough grasses and tough, spiky plants. This desolate zone, above 10,000 feet (3,048 meters), is called the

Tree ferns grow in a subtropical forest, which is about 4,000-feet (1,219-meters) high.

páramo. Typical of this region are the espeletias, known as *frailejones*, with bright yellow flowers. Spaniards gave the plants this name, which means "tall friars," because they grow to about 6 feet (1.8 meters). Lupins and gentians also add a touch of purplish blue to the alpine landscape.

Below this level, but still in a cool atmosphere and often covered in mist, grows a subtropical or temperate forest. Here the vegetation is densely tangled with tree ferns, bamboos, and palms among which passionflowers, orchids, and other blossoms flourish.

At a lower level still, and according to the rainfall, there may be either a rich tropical forest or a drier forest of tough trees, cactus, and thorny scrub.

In places along the coast, in Lake Maracaibo and in the Orinoco

Venezuela's national flower, the orchid, (left) and national tree, the araguaney (right)

Delta, there are mangrove forests that provide a very rich habitat for aquatic life.

Forests in the south, in Guiana, and the Amazonas territory are mostly tropical rain forest. In the hot and very humid conditions, trees grow tall. They are supported by wide buttress roots as they reach to the canopy; their trunks are bare for sixty feet (eighteen meters) or more and from the branches grow a tangle of other plants—lianas, stranglers, and vines.

Venezuela is famed for its variety of orchids, and the national flower is a deep lilac-pink orchid.

The national tree is the bright-yellow flowering araguaney that grows almost everywhere in the republic.

To preserve its great variety of flora and fauna, Venezuela has created over thirty-two national parks in different parts of the country. The first, the Henri Pittier Park, was founded in 1937 on the Caribbean coast. It incorporates a profile from sea level to 7,973 feet (2,430 meters), including flora from lower tropical, subtropical, and temperate zones.

Some of Venezuela's animals are the capybara (top left), the jaguar (above), and the tapir (bottom left).

FAUNA

Most of the wildlife is found in the forests of the south where it has been allowed to survive without much disturbance.

Among the native animals are many that are found in rain forest everywhere in South America. These include jaguars, pumas, and ocelots—all members of the cat family. Monkeys of many different species live in the forest canopy and the distinctive roaring of groups of howler monkeys can be heard for miles around.

The heaviest animal of the forest, weighing up to 300 pounds (136 kilograms) is the tapir, and the largest rodent is the capybara, which is semiaquatic and the size of a small pig. Other animals hunted by the Indians for food are deer, sloths, anteaters, and peccaries, or wild pigs.

The Orinoco crocodile is the largest in South America. They

A giant anteater (above) and an anaconda (right)

have been under threat from hunters for many years, though
protection is at last having results. But it will be many years
before they are seen in the numbers reported by von Humboldt. It
was almost two hundred years ago when he wrote saying the
crocodiles in the Orinoco "swarmed like worms in the shallow
waters of the river."

There are many other reptiles, including iguanas, and some
venomous snakes like the bushmaster, fer-de-lance, coral snake,
and rattlesnake. There are many nonvenomous species, such as
the boa constrictor and anaconda, which reaches a length of 25
feet (7.6 meters).

The Canaima National Park in Guiana has been created around
the tepuis of the Gran Sabana in the region of Angel Falls. Within
this park there are four species of animals particularly in need of
protection. They are the giant anteater, the giant brazilian otter,
the jaguar, and the giant armadillo.

The great blue heron (above), the scarlet ibis (above right), and the whistling tree duck (right) are just a few of the interesting birds found in Venezuela.

Many species of fish live in the Orinoco and its tributaries. Among the largest are catfish, which feed on the murky riverbed and reach a weight of 200 to 300 pounds (90 to 136 kilograms). Of the denizens of these rivers, two mammals are well known—the river dolphin and the freshwater manatee. The Indian tribes believe the river dolphin has magical powers. Also the Indians have legends about the freshwater manatee, a relative of the sea cow or mermaid of old. It browses on underwater grasses and suckles its young.

BIRDS

Among the many bird species, parrots, herons, toucans, and macaws are native to the tropical forest that are alive with their calls. Each of these birds has its own specific food. Hummingbirds, the tiny fast, wing-beating jewels of the forest, use their long bills to take nectar and insects from flowers.

One of the most extraordinary birds, which is restricted to a very specific habitat and food, is the *guácharo*, or oilbird. This curious bird lives in caves in forested places. Von Humboldt wrote about the oilbirds of a cave near Cumaná, where the Indians collected the young birds from nests on the ledges and boiled them to release large quantities of oil. The principal food of the adult bird is a rich, oil palm fruit that they take at night when they set out from their cave. The Cave of the Guácharos is now a national park and a great tourist attraction.

The flooded lands are some of the richest for birds, the mangroves and the Llanos being most famous. Large numbers of herons, egrets, and scarlet ibis gather in these places, together with migrants such as the whistling ducks, on their way north or south from the Caribbean and North America.

Chapter 3

PREHISTORY, CONQUEST, AND INDEPENDENCE

EARLY TRIBES

People arrived in South America some time between 10,000 and 20,000 B.C. They almost certainly came from Asia, crossing the Bering Strait toward the end of the Ice Age, before making their way south through North and Central America.

The first inhabitants of Venezuela were hunters and some fragments of their stone tools have been found on a site near Coro. Archaeologists have dated the tools at around 12,000 to 14,000 B.C. But apart from a few finds like these, there is little other evidence to show how the people lived.

Early people may have arrived in time to hunt the last of the very large animals, like the mastodon and giant sloth. Then, after these animals became extinct, hunters sought smaller game and fish. In time the people became more settled, and by 1000 B.C. some of the hunters had become simple farmers.

By the time the Spaniards arrived in the early sixteenth century, the most advanced of the farming groups were the Indians who lived in the Venezuelan Andes, particularly the Timotes tribe.

Pre-Columbian Indian carvings found at Chichiriviche

They used irrigated terraces to grow maize and potatoes. They made attractive pots and urns.

Less developed, and living partially nomadic lives, were the Indians of the lowlands and the rivers. Using slash-and-burn methods to clear the ground, they cultivated manioc, which was their staple food. They supplemented their diet with meat from forest animals like tapirs, monkeys, rodents, and snails and fish from the rivers.

Cotton was known to many of the tribes and was used to make hammocks. Some fruit trees were cultivated, cocoa beans were crushed to make a drink, and tobacco was used as a medicine. Common to most tribes were bows and arrows for hunting; musical instruments, such as drums and flutes made of wood, bone, and shell; and dugout canoes for use at sea, as well as on the rivers. Unknown to all tribes, however, was any form of writing, metals, or the wheel.

The largest concentrations of Indians were in Paria in the east, west of Lake Maracaibo, and in the Andes. While in the remote, inaccessible parts of the south, very primitive food-gathering groups remained isolated and unaffected by the arrival of the Europeans.

THE FIRST SPANIARDS

Christopher Columbus reached the South American mainland for the first and only time on his third voyage in 1498. A wooden cross on the beach at Puerto Colón commemorates his visit. He made some explorations along the coast, noted that the native Indians were decorated with pearls, and then left.

In the following year an expedition led by Alonso de Ojeda and Amerigo Vespucci (after whom America was named) arrived. It was this expedition that saw the stilted houses from which Venezuela got its name.

The Spanish explorers who followed were initially interested in two things. First they hoped to make their fortunes, either by finding the legendary El Dorado or by trading pearls, gold, and brazilwood, which was valued in Europe for its red dye. Secondly they needed slaves to work on sugarcane plantations in the Caribbean islands.

The pearl trade led to the first European settlement in South America in 1509. It was on a barren island called Cubagua off the Venezuelan coast. Although there was neither fresh water nor supplies on Cubagua, the population grew from three hundred in 1520 to fifteen hundred in 1535. Supplies were carried from the nearby island of Margarita and the mainland town of Cumaná, founded in 1521. But the pearl oyster beds were soon exhausted and by 1550 Cubagua was abandoned.

The slaving raids created a good deal of hostility among the Indian peoples of the coast, who in later years fought determinedly against attempts by the Spanish to settle in the coastal highlands.

To the west, the town of Coro was founded in 1527. A year later, in return for a loan, Charles V of Spain granted the German

Barquisimeto (left) and Valencia (right)

banking house of Welser the right to explore the regions around
Coro. Anxious to make the most of this opportunity, the Welsers
undertook some intrepid expeditions over the Sierra de Perijá
mountain range into Colombia, into the Llanos as far south as the
Meta River, and along the coast. Though they did not find El
Dorado, they greatly improved the geographical knowledge of the
area. However, as ruthless pioneers, they treated the Indians badly
and increased local hostility to European settlement.

The Spaniards realized that, if they were to successfully colonize
the territory, they had to establish permanent towns. They
relinquished the dream of El Dorado in favor of a more realistic
economy based on cattle and mining.

Between 1545 and 1553 the towns of El Tocuyo, Barquisimeto,
and Valencia were established. But Indian resistance prevented
any farther advance east of Valencia, particularly into the valley
where the Caracas Indians lived. Several small Spanish
expeditions failed, and it was not until 1567 that Diego Losada,

with a thousand men, succeeded in founding the city of Caracas. Indian resistance continued to the east and south and ceased only in 1580 when an epidemic of smallpox devastated the Indian population.

SPANISH GOVERNMENT

For the purpose of administering its colonies in Spanish America, the Spanish crown appointed viceroys, one based in Mexico and one in Lima, Peru. The vast territory each was in charge of was called a viceroyalty. At a later date two other viceroyalties were created, one based in Bogotá, Colombia, and one in Buenos Aires, Argentina. For most of the colonial period, Venezuela was part of the viceroyalty of Peru.

The basic unit of the viceroyalty was a province. Provincial governors were appointed who were responsible only to the viceroys, but they were advised in military, financial, and other matters by an *audiencia*—a form of high court with certain administrative functions.

The first province of Venezuela was centered on Coro where the governor lived. After 1577 the governor lived in Caracas. Other provinces were gradually created and in 1777 they were all grouped into the new captaincy-general of the provinces of Venezuela.

Each town in the province had a *cabildo*, or town council, made up of the most influential traders and landowners in the district. Being in a position to control local prices and investment, they were a powerful body. The cabildo was also the only part of government in which the local people took part.

COLONIZATION AND SETTLEMENT

Economically the new colony relied on its agricultural produce and some mining. The Spaniards introduced some crops, including wheat and some citrus fruits, which together with sugarcane, rice, coffee, cocoa, and cotton grew well in the warm valleys of the mountains.

The Spaniards also brought in sheep and pigs, as well as cattle and horses that thrived in the Llanos. Thousands of animals roamed the grasslands and a lucrative export trade in hides and skins developed.

To organize a work force, the Spanish crown authorized the use of the *encomienda* system, whereby grants of the land coupled with a band of Indians were given to a Spanish soldier or settler. In return, the Indians were supposed to be cared for, materially and spiritually. But this did not happen and the majority of Indians became slaves and were treated badly. In Venezuela the encomienda did not survive into the seventeenth century because of the death of so many Indians in the smallpox epidemic.

In the conquest of new colonies, priests accompanied the Spanish soldiers. As early as 1513, Franciscan and Dominican missionaries had founded monasteries on the coast. These missions ended in disaster, but the Franciscans successfully established convents in most important towns by the middle of the seventeenth century.

Most teaching and education in the seventeenth and eighteenth centuries was done by priests and missionaries. They built many libraries and schools. Another branch of the Franciscans, together with Jesuits and Capuchin missionaries, took up the challenge of

*Left: A mestizo girl   Right: A Spanish fortress built in 1599
to prevent the British from entering Venezuela to search for gold.*

the Llanos, the Orinoco Basin and Guiana. Often exploring alone
in wilderness where no other European had been, among hostile
Indians, and in extreme heat, the missionaries founded many
settlements and towns. Much of their work was subsequently
destroyed in the struggle for independence, but their conquest of
the interior completed the task of colonization and helped to
define the territory that would become the Republic of Venezuela.

COLONIAL SOCIETY

When the Spaniards first arrived in South America, few brought
wives with them. Instead they married the local people, and so the
part-Spanish, part-Indian, *mestizo* was born. The people of mixed
blood were generally poor, but free. They were craftsmen,
artisans, and shopkeepers.

African slaves were brought in to work in the pearl fisheries
and on the sugarcane plantations. Socially African slaves and

native Indians were considered to be the lowest class, although slaves were treated better than in other parts of South America. If they could get the money, they could buy their freedom.

The whites of colonial society comprised the *Creoles*, Spaniards born in the colony, and the *Peninsulares*, Spaniards from Spain who settled in the colony. The Peninsulares, regarded as representatives of the Spanish crown, held most of the positions of authority, and this was resented by the Creoles, who were landowners, and usually very wealthy. Creoles were allowed to be members of the cabildos, and few Peninsulares could not afford to ignore their local power.

As a result of trade, particularly in the eighteenth century, some Basques from Spain become influential in Venezuelan colonial society. They bought land, settled with their families, and became part of the governing class.

TRADE

From the outset Spain tried to prevent the new colony from trading with other European countries, but distance and the cost of defending her possessions made this difficult.

For some foreigners the lure of gold or silver was still strong, and the coast of Venezuela was subject to attack during most of the seventeenth century by buccaneers like the British adventurer, Henry Morgan.

Mostly, though, Europeans were interested in the more ordinary items of trade. The Dutch, for example, needed a good supply of salt, which they found on the peninsula of Araya opposite Cumaná. Also in demand by Dutch, French, and English traders were the high-quality tobacco from the Andean slopes, excellent cocoa from the Caracas valley, and other commodities such as wheat, hides, and cotton. The colonists used the money they earned from the illegal trade to buy manufactured goods and to purchase slaves for the plantations.

Trading and contraband continued to be illegal until 1728, when King Philip V of Spain created the Caracas Company and gave it a monopoly of all trading in Venezuela. In exchange the company was to stop all smuggling. The company was run by Basque officials. Predictably the traders in the colony deeply resented the loss of their businesses, and they rebelled. Eventually in 1785 the company was forced to close, and all trade restrictions between the colony and Europe were lifted.

Trade brought the colonists into contact with revolutionary ideas and movements in Europe. The rebellion against the company was not a direct revolt against the Spanish crown, but it was an indication of the growing discontent in the Spanish colonies.

FIGHT FOR INDEPENDENCE

After the United States won its independence from Great Britain in 1776 and the French Revolution had taken place in 1789, it was the turn of the South American colonies to seek freedom from Spain.

Venezuela's first leading independence fighter was Francisco de Miranda, who lobbied hard in the United States, England, and France for support to liberate his country. But events in Europe overtook him, when King Charles IV of Spain abdicated in favor of Napoleon Bonaparte's brother Joseph. The reaction in Caracas was to depose the Spanish captain-general.

*A protrait of
Simón Bolívar*

On April 19, 1810, the cabildo of Caracas became the new government of the provinces of Venezuela and power was in the hands of the Creole class. The cabildo was supported by a group of young army officers, among whom was Simón Bolívar.

Born into an aristocratic family, Bolívar had a privileged upbringing. He was educated by private tutors and in Europe, where he mixed with leading intellectuals. He married young, but his wife died a few months later from fever. Encouraged by revolutionary ideas and offended by the ostentation of the Emperor Napoleon, he resolved at the age of twenty to liberate his country.

"I will not rest," he said, "not in body or soul, until I have broken the chains of Spain."

In 1810, Bolívar joined Miranda seeking support from Europe and from other parts of Venezuela outside Caracas. A year later an earthquake hit the Caracas region and twenty thousand people died. It happened to be Good Friday, an important Catholic holy day, and many ordinary people saw this as a punishment for their actions against the Roman Catholic Spanish crown.

A royalist uprising against the Creoles was successful, Miranda was imprisoned and later died. Bolívar was exiled—penniless.

Bolivar enlisted in the army of New Granada (present-day Colombia), and successfully led the neighboring country into battle against the Spanish crown. Then against all odds, he marched a small expeditionary army 750 miles (1,207 kilometers) over the Andes and back into Venezuela. Winning battles on the way, Bolivar arrived triumphant in Caracas in July 1813. He became dictator, and was proclaimed liberator and captain-general of the armies.

During the campaign he produced a controversial document, *War to the Death*, urging Peninsulares and Creoles to join the battle for America, or die. Many did, and apart from some local royalist insurrection, the Republic of Venezuela seemed secure.

The next threat came from a group of horsemen from the Llanos, led by the ruthless, but able, royalist supporter José Tomás Boves. There followed a series of bloody battles in which thousands died. Boves won, entered Caracas, and ousted Bolivar and many of the patriots. Boves later died from a battle wound, but by 1815 the Spaniards where once again in control.

Bolivar, exiled in Jamaica, wrote his *Letter from Jamaica* in which he appealed for help from abroad and outlined his plan for a Federation of American States. Without resources there was nothing he could do.

Eventually Bolívar was invited to return to Venezuela in 1817 at the request of the revolutionary forces there. Basing himself in Angostura (now Ciudad Bolívar) on the Orinoco River, he began to organize the foundations of a new republic with himself as

General José Antonio Páez

president, a Congress, and a new constitution, which he devised and proclaimed in a famous speech in February 1819.

Supported by mercenary soldiers from Europe, and a fighting force of men of the Llanos, led by the remarkable José Antonio Páez, Bolívar was ready. He led his two-thousand-strong army through horrendous conditions across the Llanos and once more, over the Andes. He planned first to defeat the Spaniards in New Granada, which he did at the Battle of Boyacá.

He then declared that New Granada and Venezuela, together with present-day Ecuador and Panama, should be united into the Republic of Colombia. Finally in May 1821, he prepared for the last battle against the Spaniards in Venezuela. Victory was secured at the Battle of Carabobo on June 24, 1821. Bolívar then went on to help secure the liberty of Ecuador, Peru, and Bolivia, which kept him away from Colombia for five years. All this time he was still president, the Congress having refused his resignation.

When Bolivar returned, he faced chaos and revolt. By this time a sick man, he resigned as president and headed north to the Caribbean coast. He died there, in neighboring Colombia, at the age of forty-seven, a lonely and broken man.

Chapter 4

THE NEW REPUBLIC

After the death of Simón Bolívar in 1830, the strong man in Venezuela was José Antonio Páez. He had fought alongside Bolívar, leading the tough men of the Llanos. With the people's backing, he broke away from the union with Gran Colombia and appointed himself president of the separate, totally independent Republic of Venezuela.

Páez had plenty of problems to tackle as the prolonged wars had left the country in a shaky state. Thousands of young men had been killed, the fields had not been cultivated, and trade and the economy were disrupted.

CONSERVATIVES AND LIBERALS

From 1830 to 1858 Venezuela had governments that can be loosely described as conservative and liberal. Páez, who associated with the conservatives, was president twice and the dominant political figure for almost twenty years. Under this guiding hand, a new constitution was written, with the president elected for four years.

All forms of trade were encouraged; there was investment in agriculture and road building; and the economy improved. Also, Páez supported the abolition of slavery. In 1847 he declined a third term of the presidency, instead supporting José Monagas.

At the time of his election Monagas was a conservative, but once in office, he sided with the liberals. Then he became a dictator. Despite mounting opposition and with increasing repression, he and his brother alternatively took power until 1858 when he was deposed. One good act for which José Monagas will be remembered was the freeing of some forty thousand slaves and his attempt to abolish slavery in Venezuela.

THE FEDERAL WARS

For five years after the downfall of Monagas, the republic was racked by civil war. On one side were the conservatives who favored a central government, and on the other, the liberals who supported federalism.

Federalism is the bringing together of separate states for the purpose of government, while at the same time allowing them to deal independently with their internal affairs. It was not a new concept in the republic, but it was interpreted in different ways. Some people felt it would lead to equality among all people of Venezuela. Strong local men, known as *caudillos*, hoped it would be a means by which they could gain national power.

The conflict was long and bloody. Thousands of people died, the countryside was again devastated, and there were many changes in government. In 1861 Páez again took charge, but eventually he had to concede defeat to the liberals and federalists in 1863. The country became the United States of Venezuela.

Antonio Guzmán Blanco

THE LIBERAL DICTATOR

A leader of the liberals, Antonio Guzmán Blanco, dominated Venezuelan politics from 1870 to 1888. He had first been noted as a promising young man by José Monagas. Then he spent some time in Venezuela's foreign service, traveling in North America and Europe. He made his fortune while holding various political positions in the new republic, and in 1870 he assumed power at a time when a strong man was needed to bring peace to the land.

Although in many ways a dictator, Guzmán Blanco was responsible for the introduction of many modern social reforms needed by his country.

One of his first actions was to announce a program of free public primary education and state support for secondary and higher education. Foreign professors were invited to teach in the universities and an emphasis was put on scientific subjects. He founded the Institute of Fine Arts and the Museum of Natural History.

The capitol in Caracas

A new constitution in 1872 allowed for a directly elected president and universal suffrage.

To modernize the agricultural economy, the president provided for the building of roads and railways, the construction of public works, and improved living conditions for people in the towns. Economists were employed to control government spending.

One of Guzmán Blanco's most controversial actions was against the Catholic church. Essentially he wanted to make the church more liberal and separate it from the state. He exiled the archbishop of Caracas, broke with the Vatican, and seized the funds of religious establishments. New measures then allowed for freedom of religion, civil marriage, and divorce.

Guzmán Blanco was president and dictator of Venezuela three times, from 1870 to 1877, 1879 to 1884, and 1886 to 1888. When he was not in power, he ensured that a loyal supporter took his place and exiled himself to Europe. He did this because he was convinced that the people of Venezuela always would need him. But he was overconfident and the day came when he was no longer welcome in Venezuela. He died in Paris in 1899.

General Joaquín Crespo

INTERNATIONAL DISPUTES

General Joaquín Crespo seized power in 1892. During his administration he had to deal with an old territorial dispute. It was between Venezuela and Great Britain and had started in the 1840s, soon after independence, when boundaries had not been properly defined.

The dispute concerned Venezuela's eastern border in the region of the Essequibo River, and the western border of what was at that time British Guiana. When gold was found in the region in 1877, the British renewed their claim to land that not only took in the gold mines, but also the delta of the Orinoco River.

Crespo demanded arbitration, but Britain refused to agree until persuaded to do so by the United States in 1895. The findings did not please the Venezuelans. Venezuela was entitled to keep the Orinoco Delta, but a large tract of land was awarded to Great Britain. The dispute has remained unresolved to this day.

In 1899 Crespo was succeeded by Cipriano Castro. He became

Cipriano Castro (left) and Juan Vicente Gómez (right)

involved in a claim lodged by several European nations against Venezuela, for repayment of loans and compensation for injury to people and property during revolutions.

Castro's refusal to acknowledge the claims led to the sinking of three Venezuelan gunboats, the seizure of a British merchant ship by the Venezuelans, and retaliation by the British and Germans along the Caribbean coast. The United States again intervened and Castro agreed to pay some of the claims.

THE TACHIRA DICTATORS

Cipriano Castro was the first of a series of dictators from the Andean state of Tachira who ruled the country for the next fifty-nine years, except for three years between 1945 and 1948. The most feared and autocratic of these dictators was General Juan Vicente Gómez who was in power from 1909 to 1935. Although there were at least four serious attempts to depose him, Gómez outwitted his opponents every time. By ensuring that his army and police force were strong and well cared for, and by being quite ruthless in the use of arrests, imprisonment, and assassinations, Gómez kept himself in power.

Gómez's motto was "Peace, Union, Work" and during his presidency Venezuela benefited from the peace and stability he enforced. He was fortunate that oil was discovered during his term, which brought to Venezuela undreamed-of riches. Part of the wealth was invested in agriculture, roads, railways, and port facilities, and it helped to increase domestic and foreign trade. Gómez was able to pay off the entire foreign debt and still leave a considerable sum in the treasury.

However most of the expenditure served to benefit only the wealthy landowners and traders. The majority of Venezuelans continued to live in abject poverty. The dictator paid no attention to their needs and there was no improvement in their health, housing, or educational standards. Life for the poor remained much the same despite the oil bonanza. Meanwhile Gómez made himself very rich, and when he died in 1935, he owned more land and cattle than anyone else in Venezuela.

General Eleázer López Contreras, who succeeded Gómez, surprised most people by introducing relatively liberal reforms. He allowed the work force to organize unions, released some political prisoners, and eased censorship of the press. He also devised a development plan to help with education, health, agriculture, and industry. But he did not move fast enough for the opposition, and anticipating trouble, he reverted to dictatorial methods. General Isaías Medina Angarita succeeded him and was president of Venezuela through most of World War II.

Venezuela did not actively take part in the war, but it did not remain neutral. It broke relations with Germany and its allies in

1941. Great Britain relied heavily on Venezuelan oil and the revenue from increased sales funded much-needed social facilities. At the same time, Medina Angarita allowed for greater freedom of speech and of the press, and opposition parties had the opportunity to develop openly.

Elections were due in 1945, but before they could take place, the leading opposition party, Acción Democrática joined with the military to seize power. It was an important moment in Venezuelan history, as it was the first time a political party had come to power with the support of the majority of the people. But the reform program proposed by Acción Democrática during its three years in office, was too radical for the conservatives and the military. It included a new constitution giving the vote to everyone over eighteen and direct elections of the president by the people.

A coup in 1951 put another Tachira military dictator, Major Marcos Pérez Jiménez, in power. Using methods similar to his predecessors, Pérez Jiménez imprisoned the opposition, silenced the press, and concentrated his government's efforts on public works in Caracas and on industrial projects. He, too, made himself very rich. By 1958 the opposition was strong enough to force Pérez Jiménez into exile. The people demanded a democratic government.

DEMOCRATIC GOVERNMENT

In 1959 Acción Democrática, with Rómulo Betancourt as president, was returned to power and set up a coalition government with the Christian Democrat party. Venezuela has had democratic government ever since.

Rómulo Betancourt

Essentially the two parties have similar aims. In 1959 they set out to create the social reforms necessary to improve the life of poor people in Venezuela, and they undertook measures to modernize industry and agriculture. Inevitably there were opponents to this reform, but despite several antigovernment coups, Acción Democrática stayed in power and won the next election in 1964.

The new president was Raúl Leoni. Helped by renewed prosperity from the oil and iron industries, Leoni was able to continue the social development plans. And in 1969, for the first time in Venezuelan history, one political party peacefully transferred power to another when the Christian Democrats were elected. Throughout the 1970s and the 1980s, the two parties have alternately held office.

Recent policies have included the nationalization of banks and the oil and iron industries. After the 1973 Arab-Israeli War and the subsequent world rise in oil prices, the Acción Democrática government had the resources to implement many of its plans. The Christian Democrats claim the money was not well spent and did little for the poor.

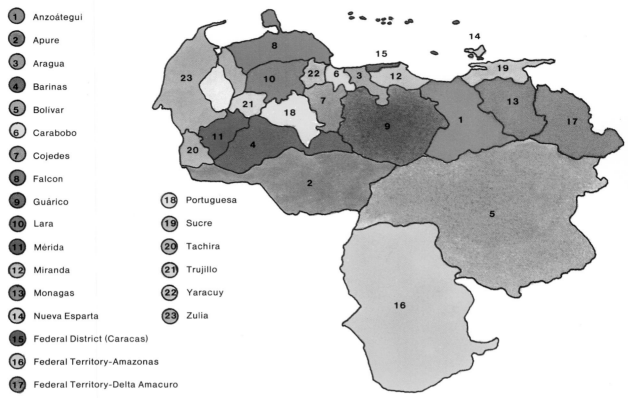

1. Anzoátegui
2. Apure
3. Aragua
4. Barinas
5. Bolívar
6. Carabobo
7. Cojedes
8. Falcon
9. Guárico
10. Lara
11. Mérida
12. Miranda
13. Monagas
14. Nueva Esparta
15. Federal District (Caracas)
16. Federal Territory-Amazonas
17. Federal Territory-Delta Amacuro
18. Portuguesa
19. Sucre
20. Tachira
21. Trujillo
22. Yaracuy
23. Zulia

Dr. Jaime Lusinchi of Acción Democrática won the 1983 election. Politicians in Venezuela today face a different problem. The 1986 collapse in the world price of oil has led to severe inflation and mounting international debts. In 1988, Carlos Andrés Pérez was elected president.

GOVERNMENT

The federal Republic of Venezuela is made up of twenty states, two federal territories, seventy-two islands in the Caribbean organized as federal dependencies, and a federal district, which includes the capital, Caracas. Each state has a governor appointed by the president and elected councils with representatives from each district. In the capital of each district there is a municipal council responsible for public services and local development.

Since independence, Venezuela has had several constitutions. The most recent, introduced by President Betancourt in January 1961, still stands.

By its terms, executive power is vested in the president who is elected for a five-year term and cannot serve twice consecutively. The president is head of the armed forces and he appoints and dismisses the council of ministers.

Congress represents the legislative power and is divided into two chambers: the Senate and the Chamber of Deputies. Two senators are elected to represent each state and two to represent the federal district of Caracas. Other senators can be elected to represent minorities and former presidents are life members of the Senate.

Deputies also are elected with a minimum of two from each state and one from each federal territory, though the number is based on one representative per fifty thousand people.

The judiciary is represented by the Supreme Court of Justice, whose members are appointed by Congress and the attorney general, who is appointed by the president.

Everyone over the age of eighteen has a vote. The seat of government is in Caracas.

NATIONAL DEFENSE

In 1986 the armed forces numbered about 50,000 men. Thirty-four thousand were enrolled in the army, 10,000 in the navy, including 4,250 marines, and 5,000 in the air force. All men eighteen to forty-five are expected to serve two years of military service.

Each municipality has its own police force.

Chapter 5

THE PEOPLE
OF VENEZUELA

The population of Venezuela, about eighteen million, is small in relation to the size of the country. Part of the reason is that large tracts of territory, like the Llanos and the Federal Territory of Amazonas are either used for cattle, or are difficult lands in which to settle. The greatest concentration of the population is in the coastal highlands, and over 85 percent of the people live in towns.

Of the original people whom Columbus called "Indians," not many true descendents have survived. Those who did, live mostly in less accessible areas, where in some cases they have remained isolated from civilization.

Thousands of Indians died during the colonial years and the Indian identity also largely disappeared when marriage with the Spaniards led to the creation of the mestizo, which now is the largest group in Venezuela.

Other elements introduced into Venezuelan society were the African slaves brought over to work the plantations in the eighteenth century. When Africans married with Europeans, they produced the *mulatto,* and today Africian and mulatto communities live mainly along the Caribbean shore and in the coastal highlands.

Compared with other countries in South America, there was relatively little immigration from Europe or elsewhere into Venezuela until the middle of the twentieth century. Then, the prosperity created from oil and the need for labor in industry attracted people from Europe and other parts of South America.

A breakdown of the Venezuelan population gives 70 percent mestizo or mixed blood, 20 percent white, 8 percent blacks (African or mulatto), and 2 percent Indian.

HISPANICS

Hispanic culture and tradition have been strongly present in Venezuela since the Spaniards first arrived in 1500. For many years until well into the twentieth century, authority and wealth was confined to a small white elite of Spanish families. Their allies in commerce were the Basques, who for some years monopolized Venezuelan trade, and Basque names are still present in today's society.

A family from the Guiana highlands

IMMIGRANTS

Just a few, though very successful, Venezuelan families and
businessmen can trace their roots to immigrant ancestors who
arrived from Europe in the early nineteenth century. Usually they
were enterprising entrepreneurs working on their own. One
exception was the community established by German Catholics in
1842 in Colonia Tovar. In a valley not far from modern Caracas,
from their alpine-styled wooden chalets, the townfolk trade
Bavarian sausages, ham, and cheese. German is spoken in homes
and restaurants.

Significant immigration began in Venezuela when several
thousand intellectuals, politicians, and scholars left Europe in the
1930s and 1940s after the Spanish Civil War. They quickly
integrated into their new life, entering universities, working in
government, and practicing as doctors and lawyers. Their new
environment inspired contributions to literature, history, and the
arts. The greatest wave of immigrants began in the 1950s, invited

by President Pérez Jiménez to help modernize Venezuela. Between 1950 and 1971, almost one million Spanish, Italian, and Portuguese arrived.

Revenue from oil and increasing prosperity for the first time, made the South American republic attractive to would-be settlers from Europe. Many of them went into the construction business where there were good profits to be made, particularly in the building boom in the capital. Others went into the retail trade.

Immigrants from neighboring Colombia also flooded across the border in search of jobs and higher salaries. Many headed for the cities and the construction industry, while others stayed in the Andes and around Maracaibo to work on farms and with cattle. They provided the labor force that Venezuela never had. Today an estimated 400,000 to 500,000 foreigners, mostly from Colombia, are working illegally in Venezuela.

THE MIDDLE CLASS

The middle class is made up of the mixed-blood population and immigrants. A middle class only emerged in Venezuela with the development, progress, and political needs of the twentieth century.

Until the beginning of the twentieth century, Venezuela had an agricultural economy. The discovery of oil created a demand for industrial and construction workers, though the executive and administrative jobs continued to be held by foreigners or a local elite who were close to President Gómez.

After his death in 1935, the rather more liberal attitude of his two successors led to a strengthening of the middle groups who helped to found the first of the political parties in opposition to

Teenagers in the market (left) and a young boy with his prize possession

the dictatorial governments. Professional associations were created, and after World War II, the middle classes demanded a greater share in the country's wealth and in making national decisions.

The democratic governments since 1959, the prosperity created by oil revenues, the construction boom, the great numbers of people now living in cities especially in Caracas, and the nationalization of the oil industry have contributed to the growth of Venezuela's middle class.

INDIANS OF VENEZUELA

The main surviving groups of forest and river Indians live in the Federal Territory of Amazonas and the Orinoco Delta and Basin. They belong to the Carib and Arawak groups and have reached different levels of development.

The Yanomani Indians live simple lives.
Left: This man holds a bow and arrow used for catching
game. Right: Indians fill baskets with cassava from
their garden in preparation for a feast.

Some tribes may still be hidden in remote parts where they have not yet been contacted, but this is unlikely to be the situation for long. As the wilderness is gradually opened up for settlers, who clear the forest and build roads, Indian survival is under threat.

Essentially Indian life is simple. The people live by hunting, fishing, and gathering food. The men move up and down the rivers by canoe, searching game that they take with their bows and arrows. The women keep gardens close to their huts, where they grow manioc (cassava), their staple food, and plantains and bananas.

A typical tribe are the Yanomani, also called Waikas, who have always resisted intrusion from outsiders. They are skilled in warfare, using wooden clubs, and they frequently have fights between themselves. Like many tribes they paint their bodies with dyes from forest plants, and they believe in the use of an hallucinogenic drug to call up spirits.

Traditional Yanomani Indian adornment (left) and a young Yanomani girl in a sewing class (right) at a mission school

Tribes who have contact with missionaries or settlers include the Pemones from Guiana and the Maquiritares from Amazonas. The Pemones have an agricultural economy, but also work as miners. Their population is thought to be increasing. The Maquiritares, who are also agriculturalists, live along the riverbanks, but are best known for their ethnic handicrafts.

In the Orinoco Delta the Warao Indians live along the riverbanks, where originally they were fishermen and hunters. There are thought to be about fifteen thousand Warao and they are said to be so adapted to their surroundings that they know how to swim and work a canoe before they learn to walk. They have canoes of different sizes, but the largest can be thirty-four feet (ten meters) long, and carry forty to fifty people. Today the Warao work in agriculture and grow rice, but they also still make use of the trees around them. Particularly the moriche palm,

Warao Indians from the Orinoco Delta
Left: A man cooks venison
Right: A busy mother prepares palm fibers
for weaving a hammock

which provides them with a form of flour from the trunk, larva that they eat, a sap that they turn into a drink, and the pulp of the fruit that is a favorite dish.

A small number of Indians, generally known as Motilones, have survived in the Sierra de Perijá west of Lake Maracaibo. Since early in the nineteenth century, having been treated badly by whites, they have been hostile to anyone entering their territory. As their home is in the region of the oil fields, it was inevitable that some oilmen would become their victims. Since 1960, however, relations have improved.

THE GUAJIRO INDIANS

Another exceptional group of Indians in Venezuela are the Guajiro. They live on the Guajira Peninsula and around Maracaibo and have their own language. They number about fifty thousand, which is an estimated half of the total Indian population in Venezuela.

Left: Guajira women in the marketplace
Right: Young Indians in their boats on the Orinoco Delta

On the peninsula, the Indians live seminomadic lives, caring for their cattle, while searching for food and water, a problem in this arid region. Sometimes families settle permanently if they find a good water supply, but generally homes are simple and temporary. The women spin and weave just as they have for centuries, and they help with the milking of the cattle and making cheeses.

Despite their contact with white people since the Spaniards first arrived, the Guajiro have shown that they can adapt to a different culture, at the same time keeping their own identity.

This is nowhere more obvious than among the Guajiro who live in the suburbs of Maracaibo, where they have integrated into city life. It is always possible to recognize the Guajiro women by their long colorful dresses and attractive headgear. They are among the poorer level of society, although some work in the oil and construction industries. The Guajiros regularly trade through their markets, selling fruit, vegetables, and hand-rolled cigars.

Housing in Caracas has marked contrasts.
Top: Middle-class apartments and,
in the background, housing for the poor.
Above: A wealthy home just outside of Caracas
Left: A close-up of the one of the homes in
the not-so-wealthy district of Caracas

Chapter 6

LIVING, LEARNING,
AND WORKING

COUNTRY OF CONTRASTS

Venezuela can be described as a country of two worlds. Most of the major cities are situated north of the Orinoco River, efficiently linked by a good road network.

In the south, in Guiana and the Federal Territory of Amazonas, people have hardly begun to touch the wilderness. There is a great gap between cities like Caracas, Valencia, and Maracaibo, and small villages and settlements in the interior.

The life of an office worker and commuter in the city is very different from that of the cattlemen of the Llanos. Outside the cities there may be less noise and pollution, but there is also less education and fewer jobs.

In the cities there is a marked contrast between rich and poor. Many thousands of people have moved from country districts into the towns in search of a better way of life. But unable to find work, they simply swell the numbers of poor living in simple brick shacks called *ranchos* on the outskirts of the towns. This is particularly evident in Caracas.

Modern multilane highway near Caracas (left) and
offices and residential buildings (right) in midtown Caracas

In the 1960s, funded by huge oil revenues, Caracas was transformed into South America's most modern capital. Small, tiled colonial buildings were replaced by high-rise glass-and-concrete structures, green hillsides gave way to sprawling residential suburbs and multilane highways now cut through the city. The population of the city rose from 1,500,000 in 1961 to 4,000,000 in 1986.

WORKING

The movement from country to town has led to many fewer people working in agriculture. In the Andean regions, there are small farmers working plots on the hillsides just as they always have. And in the Llanos, herdsmen continue to watch cattle. But today, only 16 percent of the people are employed as agricultural workers.

Many more people now work in manufacturing, service industries, and in commerce. In Caracas there are factories

*A police woman directs traffic in Mérida (left).
In Maracaibo, a construction gang builds new
middle-class housing (right)*

producing processed foods, leather and hides, glass, chemicals and pharmaceutical goods, and many other useful items for the domestic market.

Workers travel to and from factories daily, averaging a forty-hour week, with many doing night shifts for which they receive better pay. Caracas is also the center for the construction industry, in which skilled workers and laborers are employed. Workers can join trade unions, the largest being the Confederation of Venezuelan Workers, which has over 1,500,000 members.

The oil industry employs less than 2 percent of the work force, but since nationalization, Venezuelans have taken over jobs previously held by foreign technicians.

Executives and top managers in the cities work in modern air-conditioned offices, using the most up-to-date computer and communication equipment.

With increased educational opportunities, more women are finding work. When President Herrera Campíns was elected in 1979, he created a new ministry called the Participation of Women in Development.

EDUCATION

During the three hundred years of colonial rule, schools were run by the church and often attached to monasteries. Not many ordinary children went to school, as learning was the privilege of the powerful and wealthy. The very rich arranged for their children to be taught privately at home, by tutors who were usually members of the clergy. Education was only for boys. Girls were expected to stay at home and take care of their domestic duties.

President Guzmán Blanco was the first to provide schooling for the general public in 1870. He is quoted as saying that "Wherever ten children can be gathered together, there must be a schoolmaster teaching them to read and write and the first four rules of arithmetic; if there is no schoolhouse, the school must function even in the shade of some tree, in order that there shall be no Venezuelan who cannot read the Constitution of the Republic."

However, it was not until almost one hundred years later that education became a real priority of government. Since 1960 there has been a great expansion in the number of schools, with many built in towns in the interior. The government took measures to provide for more teachers.

Today in Venezuela schooling is compulsory and free for all children between the ages of seven and fifteen. Government figures from 1984 state that 78 percent of all school-age children attended school. For some children it is difficult to go to school, as in rural areas long distances may be involved, and within some poor families parents prefer the children to work to help earn money. The number of people who can read and write has

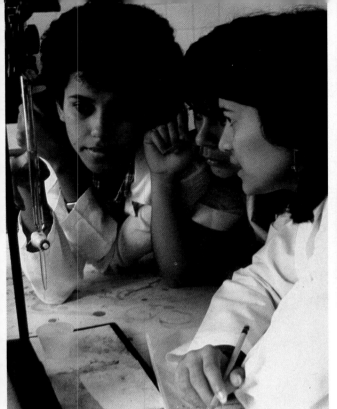

University students confer in a chemistry lab (left); a computer class (right)

improved, and now over 85 percent of the population is said to be literate.

In the 1982-83 academic year, almost 300,000 students received higher education at the university and polytechnic level. Venezuela has both state and private universities, and among the most important are three in Caracas. The largest and oldest is the Central founded in 1721, which can take about 60,000 students. The youngest, founded in 1970, is the Simón Bolívar, which as the "university of the future" is science-oriented. The third is the small, private Catholic Andrés Bello University.

To cope with the increasing need for technically skilled students, the University of the Oriente was specifically created in 1960 and in the 1970s a National Training Institute was established. At the same time a government-sponsored scholarship program sent several thousands of students overseas for technical training.

The cathedral in Mérida

THE CHURCH

The majority of Venezuelans are Roman Catholic, although there is freedom to practice any religion. In Caracas there are two Protestant churches.

Christianity was introduced into Venezuela by the Spaniards. But because the population was small and poor, fewer priests were sent there than to Mexico or Peru. Missionaries worked in many parts of the country, defying horrendous conditions to make contact with remote tribes, whom they tried to convert and educate. The church was most active in teaching and creating centers of education.

The first archbishopric in Venezuela was not established until 1804. In 1870 the church lost much of its power when President Guzmán Blanco broke with the Vatican. Relations were to some extent restored under President Gómez, who needed the support of the church and so he encouraged religious education. The church supports private education, and was one of the founders of the prestigious Catholic University in Caracas. This has brought them into conflict with the democratic governments since 1960, who support state education.

Church services are regular and well attended in Venezuela. By contrast, the Indians of the forest still keep their pagan beliefs in a world of spirits.

New churches have been built and one outstanding example of recent modern ecclesiastic architecture is the cathedral in Barquisimeto.

FOOD

In a country with many immigrants and regional differences, the food has plenty of variety. The staples of meat from the Llanos and fish from the Caribbean are eaten in most major towns, as they are transported widely.

Some cuts of beef are prepared stuffed with carrots, onions, garlic, and fat bacon or pork. The *muchacho*, as the dish is called, is sliced and is often more tender and flavorsome than the original cut. It is served with boiled black beans, or *caraotas*, and rice. Garlic and coriander are favorite seasonings. Beef is often barbecued over charcoal or oven cooked in the traditional way. A salad in Venezuela may contain crisp American-style lettuce, an ingredient almost unknown elsewhere on the continent.

But as well as internationally styled food, there are less familiar dishes, such as the flat maize pancakes, or *cachapas*, prepared as a doughlike mixture and then cooked on an iron griddle pan. Cachapas can be filled with savory mixtures or cheese, and are sold often at the roadside. Another maize based breadlike patty is

Fishermen unloading their catch (left);
a typical fruit and vegetable market in downtown Maracaibo

the *arepa*, which when plain can be unappetizing, but it makes a simple meal when complete with a filling. Arepas are typical of market stalls or street-corner shops where they are served in a simple paper wrapping.

A Christmas variation of the maize pancake is the *hallaca* stuffed with chicken, pork, olives, and spices. They are boiled in a banana or plantain leaf, which doubles as the wrapping until they are served.

A typical country meal is a *sancocho*, or stew of meat, maize, yucca, and other vegetables, often served in a large bowl with freshly made arepas alongside.

Of the unusual food, possibly some of the most striking is served in Arab restaurants in Caracas, where such dishes as chickpea *hommus* and traditional sweatmeats are indistinguishable from those of the Middle East. At the same time Venezuelans are equally at home with hamburgers and American-style sandwich bars.

THE FAMILY

The family unit in Venezuela is strong, particularly among the lower-income groups. A large family can help each other economically, and it is not unusual for three generations to live in one family house. Grandparents are taken care of, while they help by looking after the young children. Most other members of the family, apart from the school-age children, can then go out to work.

In poor families, the children frequently help to earn money, either by doing odd jobs, such as cleaning cars in the cities or in rural areas, where they assist on the land.

Among the upper-income groups, there is more freedom for families to take up individual interests. Even so, young girls lead a sheltered life compared with their counterparts in the United States or Europe.

HEALTH CARE

Health care was not taken seriously until the middle of the twentieth century and the election of democratic governments. Presidents Betancourt and Gallegos both aimed to improve the standard of living particularly of the working class and rural families. The ministry of health was given more money to spend. There was an increase in the number of hospitals and small clinics built in rural areas. Priority was given to water supplies, electricity, child care, and nutrition.

The first electrical power reached Caracas in 1897, but many towns and villages were still without it in 1945.

With the creation of the Venezuelan Development Corporation

The pollution from congested traffic in urban areas, and industrial complexes throughout Venezuela, is creating great health hazards.

in 1946, the production of crops such as sugar, cotton, and rice improved considerably, and a high percentage of the people could get reasonably balanced diets. Free school meals were introduced for children.

Malaria and other tropical diseases generally have been eradicated.

The growth in population has been rapid since 1960. This has been partly due to immigration, but also to improved standards of health and a raise in the birthrate. This increase has caused problems, making the importation of some foodstuffs necessary. It also has led to a great demand on government health and hospital services. Today over half the population is under thirty years old.

As a result of recent government legislation, workers can now receive benefits when they have an accident or are ill. Many people are concerned now that the increasing numbers of cars and factories, particularly in Caracas, will cause severe pollution and create a health hazard.

A block of new apartment buildings (left) and Parque Central complex (right) in Caracas

HOUSING

Modern, functional blocks of apartments are being built in almost every part of Venezuela. They contain bedrooms, a reception area, kitchen, bathroom, and balcony. Some have a maid's room, while others have swimming pools, depending on the income of the family buying or renting.

At the simplest level the government has a housing program to build modest apartments in the main cities and the growing industrial or mining areas. Often the housing developments are combined with government offices, shopping, sports centers, cinemas, and art galleries.

Of these, undoubtedly the most spectacular is the Parque Central complex in Caracas. Begun in 1966, it was designed to house eight to twelve thousand people (housing units range from a studio to three or four bedrooms), with space for over five hundred commercial establishments. It includes an annex to the

77

Above: A house built on stilts in a lagoon off the coast of Venezuela
Below: A traditional round house of the Yanomani Indians

A rural house perches on a hillside above Trujillo

Caracas Hilton Hotel and each of the twin glass-sided towers that dominate the complex contain fifty-five floors of offices.

The urgency in Caracas is for this type of government housing to replace the urban shanties. But people from the countryside do not always find it easy to get used to living in apartments. Many prefer the friendship of the street.

The region and available materials also influence house style. In places around Maracaibo and north in the coastal lagoons, wooden houses on stilts above the water are commonly used. They are not grand, but they are cool and away from many of the insects of the mangrove swamps.

In the Andes mountains, the houses are built in either adobe mud brick or stone and faced with a mortar of lime. Tiled or thatched, these houses are suited to the cool climate.

At the other extreme, Indians like the Yanomani live in individual "homes" protected under a large circular thatch shelter. They call it a *yano*. As many as a hundred families may live within one yano deep in the forest.

But among tribal communities closer to population centers, change is taking place, where, for example, corrugated iron is used for roofing instead of traditional thatch.

Handicrafts can be found throughout Venezuela. Clockwise from above left: hammocks sold by the roadside in Falcón, crafts from Mérida, an Indian woman working on a hammock in her market stall in Maracaibo, and woven baskets and colorful souvenirs for tourists in Caracas

Chapter 7

ARTS AND LEISURE

HANDICRAFTS

Native traditional crafts are reflected in the handicrafts made
everywhere in Venezuela. They differ according to each group
and the materials used depend on what is available locally. Heavy
woolen blankets and *ruanas*, poncholike garments open down the
front, are typical of the cooler Andean regions, as well as hats,
baskets, and *mucuras*, which are large earthenware jugs.

Following their life-style on the plains, the people of the Llanos
make saddles, ropes, harps, and a small guitarlike instrument
called a *cuatro*.

From the fishing regions of the northeast, come nets,
hammocks, and some musical instruments. Many of these items,
and others like textiles and wooden artifacts, are made for use,
though they also are traded to tourists.

MUSIC AND FIESTAS

Music developed well in colonial Venezuela, whereas there was
little in visual art. In the eighteenth century there was a school of

Devil dancers celebrating Corpus Christi (left) and musicians performing at a local feast called Dia de San Petro in Miraanda (right)

music in Caracas, and later an academy, which produced composers such as José Angel Lamas and Juan Landaeta, to whom the music of the Venezuelan national anthem is attributed. Traditional music and dance, which originated in the mixture of African, Indian, and European cultures, have survived in Venezuela through the many festivals and celebrations held throughout the year.

The festivals have both Christian and pagan significance. The best known is the celebration of Corpus Christi held in San Francisco de Yare, not far from Caracas, Devil dancers dressed in bright-red costumes and grotesque masks with two horns, celebrate outside the local Catholic church.

On the coast, pre-Lent Carnival has a Caribbean flavor with calypso music, whereas the Feast of the Turas in September in Falcón continues the rural tradition of giving thanks for a good harvest. Also in September the dances of the Negroes of San Geronomo take place in Mérida.

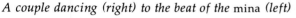
A couple dancing (right) to the beat of the mina *(left)*

A range of musical instruments is used in all festivals. They include long horns, reed flutes, the cuatro, harp, wind instruments made from deer skulls and bamboo, maracas, and drums.

The very popular *joropo* is considered the national dance. Thought to originate from the Spanish *fandango*, it has variations according to the region, but is performed in many fiestas.

In classical music, the famous Venezuelan pianist Teresa Carreño was internationally acclaimed. She gave concerts in Europe and the United States from the age of nine until her death at the age of sixty-four in 1917. The magnificent Teresa Carreño Theater, inaugurated in Caracas in 1983, is a cultural complex to honor her memory. Among its many functions, it is the home of the Simón Bolívar National Youth Symphonic Orchestra. The Ríos Reyna Hall, which holds twenty-five hundred people, was named after the first violinest and president of the Venezuelan Symphonic Orchestra. Pedro Ríos Reyna was the first to suggest a permanent base for the orchestra, which gives regular concerts of works by international and Latin American composers.

The First Festival of Latin American Contemporary Music was held in Caracas in 1977. Also in the 1970s, the Maracaibo Symphony Orchestra and the International Ballet of Caracas were founded. The ballet incorporates Venezuelan folklore and music into its repertoire.

Caracas has many concert halls and auditoriums where different forms of music can be heard, ranging from opera to rock.

MODERN ART

Toward the end of the nineteenth century, President Guzmán Blanco and his government took a positive interest in the arts and founded the National Library and the Institute of Fine Art. Following independence earlier in the century, artists were proud of their country and its history and they depicted their nationalist feelings in their paintings.

One of the best-known works of the great muralist, Martín Tovar y Tovar, shows Simón Bolívar's final victory at the Battle of Carabobo. The mural covers the ceiling in the National Capital Congress building. Other muralists of the period were Arturo Michelena and Antonio Herrera Toro.

The first great Venezuelan artist of the twentieth century was Armando Reverón, otherwise known as the "Hermit of Macuto." He was given this name because he lived like a recluse in the small coastal town of Macuto, with only his wife and a model, Juanita, for company. He was an eccentric personality, influenced both by Spanish painters and French impressionists, and his paintings were extraordinary. His work has attracted much attention since his death.

Most of Reverón's contemporaries were more conventional—

*Martín Tovar y Tovar's mural on the ceiling
in the National Capital Congress building*

painters like Manuel Cabre, Hector Poleo, and Rafael Monasterios. Cabre is famous for his painting of the Avila, the mountain that overlooks Caracas, and Monasterios is known for his landscapes, particularly those of Andean scenes.

A number of successful artists arrived with the immigrant communities. Angel Luque from Córdoba, Spain, and Louisa Richter from Germany have lived in Venezuela since 1955, and Guillermo Heiter from Czechoslovakia since 1949. Heiter is known for his religious paintings.

Venezuelan governments have supported many leading artists with grants to study in Europe.

The two most famous artists in Venezuela today are Alejandro Otero and Jesús Soto. Their individual art forms include geometric patterns, moving sculpture or kinetic art, and a particular use of color.

Among Otero's best-known works is his stainless steel arch of moving panels, the *Abra Solar* in the Plaza Venezuela in Caracas.

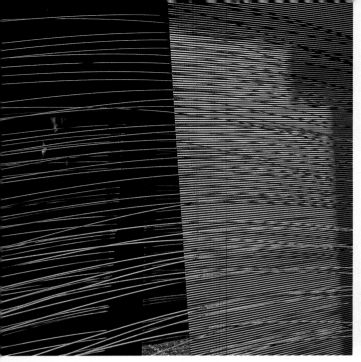

Gran Guadrato *by Jesús Soto (left) and a mobile sculpture,* Abra Solar, *by Alejandro Otero*

Soto's sculpture *Gran Guadrato* is stainless steel, with delicate metal bars moving in front of a painted background, is in the patio of the Galería Nacional de las Artes in Caracas. The slightest wind sets the whole sculpture into a shimmer of color.

Both of these men worked with Venezuela's greatest architect, Carlos Villanueva, whose first important work was the bullring in Maracay, which he built for President Gómez in 1931. In 1941 Villanueva undertook his first big public project, which was to clear a derelict part of central Caracas and replace it with a modern low-cost housing development, known today as El Silencio.

His greatest achievement was the University City of the Central University of Caracas. His design was for an open-plan campus, using activity centers, plazas and patios, gardens, covered walkways, and art. The Olympic Stadium and the Olympic Swimming Pool, one of the largest in the world, used daring designs in reinforced concrete. Most dramatic is the Great Hall

The University of the Andes in Mérida

(*Aula Magna*), and the particularly striking feature of Alexander Calder's *flying saucers*. Designed to control the acoustics, they hang like colored, floating clouds from the ceiling and walls.

As well as Otero and Soto, the works of many Venezuelan artists are represented in the University City. These include bronze sculptures by Henry Laurens, glass mosaics by Fernand Léger and Oswaldo Vigas, and works from Pascual Navarro and Armando Barrios.

LITERATURE

Before independence, most literature was in the form of Spanish chronicles or reports on the colony, and were often written by priests. These included the work of Oviedo y Baños and Padre José Gumilla.

The great man of nineteenth-century letters in Venezuela, and in South America, was the philosopher and poet Andrés Bello.

One book he wrote, a sort of guidebook and history of Venezuela, was the first book to be printed in the country. He was at one time tutor to the young Simón Bolívar and accompanied him on his mission to London in 1810. Bello never returned to Venezuela, but lived in Chile, where he was instrumental in creating that country's educational system. A central theme of Bello's work was his desire to separate the art and literature of Spanish America from that of Spain.

A contemporary intellectual of Bello's was Simón Rodriguez. He, too, was a tutor to Simón Bolívar, and his revolutionary ideas had a very profound effect on the liberator.

The post-independence years produced men like Agustín Codazzi, who wrote a geography of the country and prepared an atlas covering Venezuela's natural resources. There were also political thinkers like Fermín Toro.

The Venezuelan Academy of Literature was founded in 1872. Much of the literature from that time, and particularly in the first half of the twentieth century, has been concerned with the history and life of Venezuela. Writers such as Miguel Otero Silva tried to analyze the country's problems and looked for possible solutions.

Best known and most widely read were the works of Rómulo Gallegos. In his 1929 novel, *Doña Bárbara*, he expresses a cautious optimism for the country's future. Ten years later he was deeply involved in politics, and became president in 1947. His later novels did not have the impact of his earlier work.

Venezuelan history and contemporary problems have continued to be the theme of older writers such as Arturo Uslar Pietri and Otero Silva, as well as the new younger generation with Luis Britto García, who mixes history with fiction.

Francisco Herrera Luque is an author who has recently broken publishing records in Venezuela. His historical fiction, easy to read and appealing to the general population, has sold to millions.

FILM AND THEATER

Venezuela has a small film industry. Because of the high costs involved, and even with government subsidies, the industry has faced problems. In particular it has to compete with big-budget films from the United States, which are popular among Venezuelans. History has been a favorite subject and many films have been made from national literature. Documentaries are produced also.

Theater was the base from which filmmaking started, and two leading theater directors, Isaac Chocrón and Román Chalbaud, later became film directors.

Drama festivals in the 1960s established the theater that is still popular today. The Fifth International Festival of Theater was held in Caracas in 1981, with participants from eighteen countries.

RECREATION

Under the presidency of Carlos Andrés Pérez, a minister for youth was appointed. One of his responsibilities was to encourage sport. There are opportunities for many activities in Venezuela, such as mountain climbing, skiing, swimming, and sailing, as well as organized sports like boxing, football (soccer), basketball, and athletics.

Baseball is the national game, with teams in every part of the country. The first baseball club was formed in Caracas in 1895 by Venezuelan students returning from the United States. All

A little league baseball team (left)
and a surfer riding the waves (right)

children from five to eighteen are encouraged to play and professional teams compete to take part in the Caribbean League Baseball Championships. Most cities have modern stadiums.

Football is very popular also. Many provincial towns field teams of an international standard and a national team takes part of the World Fútbol Cup held every four years.

Boxers, such as Morochito Rodríguez and Morocho Hernández, have been particularly successful in the Olympics and in world-title fights.

The first horse race in Venezuela was run in the 1890s, and racing was established as a national sport with the construction of the first track in 1908. In Caracas, La Rinconada Racecourse has a racing program every weekend, and there are good racetracks in several other cities. Race horses compete internationally and have won several major prizes.

Venezuelan athletes have won world medals in waterskiing and motorcycling.

Chapter 8

A WEALTHY NATION

Venezuela is famous for its oil. It is the world's seventh-largest producer.

But the country is also immensely rich in other mineral and energy resources, which have not been fully exploited yet. Oil revenues have enabled Venezuela, and particularly Caracas, to modernize in the twentieth century, but the country's reliance on one source of income is also a problem. About 50 percent of government revenue is derived from oil, and the economy is hard hit when there is a drop in world prices. In recent years Venezuela has experienced inflation, unemployment, reduction in government spending, higher prices, and devaluation of the currency.

With so much wealth generated by oil, little attention has been given to agriculture until recently. For most of the 1980s, Venezuela imported as much as 50 percent of its food. Venezuela has what many economists call a "dual economy." Venezuelans involved in the oil industry live in a different economy, with a different standard of living, than Venezuelans who are not involved in the oil industry.

A "nodding donkey" oil well pumper and a gas burn off on Lake Maracaibo's shore

To pay its import bill and meet its commitments, Venezuela has to borrow from international banks and in 1987 the total foreign debt was thirty-three million United States dollars, making it the fourth-largest debtor in South America. So far Venezuela has been able to repay the interest on these loans, helped by its dollar reserves and known mineral resources. But with a decline in the reserves and an unstable world oil price, the present government anticipates difficulties.

THE PETROLEUM INDUSTRY

The symbol of oil, the "nodding donkey" pump, is a familiar sight in widely separated parts of the country. In some oil towns the machinery, pipes, and burning gas vents are set on street corners. The northeast side of Lake Maracaibo is a forest of production platforms — the cornerstone of the national economy.

The oil history of Venezuela began when the Caribbean

Petroleum Company, a subsidiary of Royal Dutch Shell, began commercial production of oil in the Lake Maracaibo Basin in 1914. Three years later Venezuela's first oil refinery was built and exports of petroleum began. The relative stability and peace enforced by President Gómez's dictatorial regime allowed the industry to develop. In 1922 a massive blowout of Number 2 Well at Los Barrosos near Lake Maracaibo confirmed that Venezuela possessed huge oil deposits. Gómez's policy was to give favorable terms to foreign investors and in 1924, American companies began to purchase concessions to drill. By 1926 petroleum was Venezuela's chief export and three years later the republic was the world's largest oil exporter.

As the industry developed, particularly after World War II, resentment toward foreign ownership and control grew. In 1976, after years of preparation, the oil industry was nationalized during the administration of President Carlos Andrés Pérez.

The national oil company, Petroleos de Venezuela (PDVSA) with its subsidiaries Corpoven, Lagoven, and Maraven, now controls the industry. It is responsible for exploration, extraction, refining, and export. PDVSA exploration has been successful in increasing Venezuela's estimated oil reserves, which at the end of 1986 were 55,521 million barrels.

The country has light, medium, and heavy crude oil, with deposits in the Maracaibo Basin, in the Eastern Venezuelan Basin, and in the western Llanos in the Apure-Barinas Basin. Exploration has been concentrated in the Gulf of Venezuela, southwest of Lake Maracaibo, and in the Orinoco. The Orinoco heavy oil belt is the largest accumulation of heavy petroleum in the world. Extracting heavy oil is difficult and expensive and only recently have economic ways of producing, processing, and transporting commercial quantities been found. But it could be centuries before the true potential is realized.

In addition to its own refineries in Venezuela, PDVSA has increased refining capacity by leasing two installations on nearby Caribbean islands.

With the sharp fall in the world oil price in 1986, PDVSA took steps to protect its international market. It bought shares in United States and European companies that refine and distribute oil. Thus by extending its refining operations internationally, Venezuela enhanced its reputation as a world producer and guaranteed outlets for its oil, particularly in times of world crisis.

Venezuela is self-sufficient in natural gas, which is often found in deposits associated with oil. Exploration of reserves in eastern Venezuela is now urgently underway. Construction has begun on a 949-mile (1,527-kilometer) pipeline between the Paria Peninsula and the industrial towns of west and north Venezuela. It is scheduled for completion in the 1990s. Natural gas is the main raw material used in petrochemicals, an industry in which Venezuela is investing heavily.

PDVSA also plans to develop the coal reserves in the Guasare coalfields in the western state of Zulia. An agreement has been reached with foreign investors, and possible developments include building a railway to carry coal to a port that would be specifically built on the Gulf of Venezuela. Most of the coal considered as good steam coal will be exported to Europe.

MINING

Venezuela has a great variety of minerals, the majority of which are located in Guiana and the Orinoco regions. They include iron

An iron ore strip mine on Cerro Bolívar

ore, bauxite, coal, gold, diamonds, zinc, copper, lead, silver, manganese, titanium, nickel, marble, sulfur, phosphates, mercury, and uranium. Most of these barely have been exploited.

Major iron-ore deposits are mined in hills south of Ciudad Bolívar, of which the most important is the Cerro Bolívar, a "hill of iron" some 7 miles (12 kilometers) long and 2.4 miles (4 kilometers) wide, towering 1,935 feet (590 meters) above the surrounding savanna. Carved into by mining operations, it resembles a pyramid. It was discovered by a team of North American geologists in 1947, but iron had been known in the region long before. Sir Walter Raleigh noted it in 1595, and Capuchin monks in the eighteenth century used it to make tools and wheels. The iron industry was nationalized in 1974 and reserves are estimated to be very large.

Greater efforts are underway to mine bauxite, which is used in the aluminum industry. Recent discoveries have revealed large deposits of high-grade bauxite, sufficient to supply the local aluminum industry entirely from Venezuelan sources.

Gold prospectors are hard at work in Guiana. Some twenty thousand wildcat operations around El Dorado, using primitive tools and living in basic conditions, are seeking to make their fortune. Not all prospectors declare what they find, but one estimate gives a yearly extraction of around 10 metric tons, worth about 250,000,000 United States dollars. The government is concerned that considerable amounts of gold are being lost due to primitive extraction methods and it plans to organize the industry.

INDUSTRY

Until 1960 the center of the manufacturing industry in Venezuela was Caracas and the Valencia Basin in the coastal highlands. In that year the government founded Ciudad Guayana at the confluence of the Orinoco and Caroní rivers opposite Puerto Ordaz, and brought together in one unit the industrial zone of Matanzas and the urban centers of Puerto Ordaz and San Felix. The intention was to create an industrial center for processing the mineral wealth of the Guiana region, and this site was chosen because large ships could use the Orinoco for access. Nearby rivers also would be a good potential source of hydroelectric energy. About a half million people now work there, living in a modern complex of high-rise apartments and fast motorways.

A government body, the Venezuelan Guayana Corporation (CVG), was created to run the development and it is the second-largest industrial group, after the oil sector, in the country. Under its control are two aluminum smelters, an alumina plant, a tractor factory, and a steel complex that includes one of the most

A steel plant on the Orinoco River

modern plants in the world, installed by the Sidor Steel Company. Sidor employs seventeen thousand workers making over one thousand different products, and it is investing heavily in new projects. The aluminum industry also is expanding rapidly and Ciudad Guayana is on course to have the biggest smelter in the world. The abundant supply of bauxite and local cheap labor, with energy supplied from nearby hydroelectric plants, will make Venezuelan aluminum highly competitive in the world market.

Venezuela's petrochemical industry is run by Pequiven, the state-owned Petroquimica de Venezuela S.A. company, which is part of PDVSA. The industry is centered in Morón on the coast 106 miles (170 kilometers) west of Caracas, and in the western state of Zulia. Products include fertilizers, explosives, insecticides, sulfuric acid, and plastics. Levels of production for 1986 were the best the company has ever achieved and expansive plans have now been formed for future investment, making use of the abundant natural gas resources.

Other manufacturing industries include electric goods,

machinery, pharmaceuticals, rubber, and car assembly. These rely to some extent on importing materials. The more traditional industries are food processing, textiles, ceramics, and paper.

All industry, and particularly construction, has been affected by a drop in consumer demand and shortage of import materials, which followed the collapse of the world oil price.

HYDROELECTRICITY

A most important factor in the development of Venezuelan industry is hydroelectricity. With many rivers able to produce an almost unlimited supply of cheap electricity, some large projects are underway.

The Guri or Raúl Leoni Dam on the Caroní River, a tributary of the Orinoco, with its mouth close to Ciudad Guayana, is the biggest. It was inaugurated in November 1986. When completed, the installation will be one of the largest in the world with a production of over ten million kilowatts of energy. That is sufficient to supply all the energy needs of Venezuela as well as some neighboring countries.

AGRICULTURE

For most of the twentieth century, farming, forestry, and fishing have been neglected because oil was more profitable. In 1960 President Betancourt's government introduced agrarian reform so that small farmers could own land and receive financial and technical assistance. But the new ownership made little difference to agriculture productivity. From 1977 the amount of land under cultivation steadily fell and food production dropped.

Plowing with buffalo power in the Andes

Commercial crops, many grown in the coastal highlands, include sugarcane, rice, maize, sorghum, cocoa, bananas, and cotton. Although Venezuela grows maize and sorghum, it still needs to import more cereals, as well as some vegetable oils and dairy products.

The main cultivated areas are around Maracay and Valencia in the coastal highlands, Barquisimeto and the western Llanos, and El Tigre in the eastern Llanos. Elsewhere small farmers grow a variety of food for their own use, such as cassava, beans, nuts, and tropical fruits.

When President Lusinchi took office in 1984 his government made the improvement of agriculture one of its top priorities. A ten-year program is underway to improve and irrigate existing agricultural land, and to get 247,000 acres (1,000,000 hectares) newly cultivated. The government is subsidizing the price of fertilizers by 50 percent. Loans with low-interest rates have been

Small farms in the Guiana highlands

made available to food producers and farmers who are exempted from paying tax also.

There has been an immediate rise in production, particularly in cereals, and the amount of land used for agriculture has increased by about one-third. There also has been a significant drop in food imports. The improvement has been called an agricultural miracle, which the government may have difficulty in sustaining because of the large subsidies involved.

The Llanos are the traditional cattle country of Venezuela, but herds are raised also in the coastal highlands and Maracaibo Basin. Breeds include the native criollo cattle, descended from the original Spanish stock, zebu from the Indian subcontinent, and European shorthorn. There are more than twelve million cattle, bred for meat and milk. Beef production has dropped recently due to the smuggling of cattle across the border to Colombia where prices are higher. Pig farming and poultry are a growing industry.

A ranch owner and his manager check the health of young pigs

FISHING

Despite the potential of its long coastline and many lakes, Venezuela's fishing industry is small. Familiar species of fish include sardines and shellfish, and recently there has been an increase in the number of tuna caught. Venezuela is becoming a major world producer.

FORESTRY

More than half of Venezuela is covered by some kind of forest and most of it belongs to the state. Ninety percent of the forests are in Guiana and are rich in hardwoods. The remainder are in the states of Apure and Barinas and the western Llanos, and where mahogany, the world's most important cabinet wood, grows. These immense resources have yet to be tapped, as Venezuela does not possess a developed timber industry.

Most of Venezuela's coffee grows in the shade of banana trees.

Chapter 9

VENEZUELA AND
THE WORLD

EXPORTS AND IMPORTS

Over 90 percent of Venezuela's export earnings come from oil. It is the world's third-largest exporter. In the first six months of 1987, Venezuela exported an average of 1.47 million barrels of oil a day, at an average cost of 16.24 United States dollars per barrel.

Aluminum is the most important non-oil export. Between 1983 and 1986, non-oil exports almost doubled, from 764 million to 1,372 million United States dollars.

Coffee grown in the Andes and coastal highlands was the most important export before oil took over in 1926, and it is still the principal food export today.

Venezuela's chief export markets are the United States, the Netherlands Antilles, Canada, and Italy. Over half the country's imports come from the United States, and the other main sources are Japan, Canada, and West Germany. Imports include machinery and transport equipment, manufactured goods, food, and chemicals.

Venezuela is interested in attracting foreign investors. The wealth of resources and energy are real incentives, but many would-be investors have been discouraged by excessive paperwork and bureaucracy. The present government is concerned with the problem, and proposing improved terms for foreign companies willing to invest in tourism, agriculture, electronics, or any business that will help the country's exports.

Another difficulty for foreign companies is the exchange rate of the Venezuelan bolívar to the United States dollar and other foreign currencies. Often there is more than one exchange rate. For example, in 1987 one rate of 7.50 bolívars to the U.S. dollar applied to "priority" imports, such as medicines and food, and another rate of 14.50 bolívars to the U.S. dollar applied to raw materials for industry. Additionally, these official rates of exchange are altered quite frequently.

TRANSPORTATION

Venezuela has a modern and efficient road network. It is possible to drive from Caracas to all the state capital cities and to many of the smaller towns. Depending on the region, whether in the mountains or crossing the Llanos, roads may be asphalt or simple dirt surfaces. About half the total network of 37,282 miles (60,000 kilometers) is asphalt or hardtop, and most roads are well maintained. Some, like Caracas to Maracay, are superhighways. There are service and gas stations on most routes.

The multilaned highway between Caracas and its airport, Maiquetia on the coast, is an impressive feat of engineering. By forging a route using tunnels through the coastal range, the journey that previously took up to four hours was cut to thirty minutes—when there are no traffic jams.

A commercial airline first began to operate in Venezuela in

*A multilane expressway in Caracas (left)
and passengers boarding a VIASA plane*

1929. It was called the Compania General Aeropostal Francesa and it used bi-motor planes on regular flights to Maracay, Maracaibo, and Ciudad Bolívar. Today, it is owned by the government and is known as Linea Aeropostal Venezolana. Part of the service it provides is to twenty-two airports in the least-populated regions, such as the Amazonas territory, Guiana, and the Amacuro Delta. For passengers and freight between the major cities, the coast, and internationally to the Netherlands Antilles and the island of Trinidad, it uses modern jets.

Another Venezuela air company is AVENSA, which is privately owned. Two small airlines, Aeronaves del Centro and Aero-Ejecutivos operate on domestic routes only.

International flights between Venezuela and other capital cities in South America and Europe are covered by the national company, VIASA. Major airlines from the United States and Europe have many regular flights to Venezuela.

In addition to the big airlines, there are many small companies with "air taxis" and helicopters that operate in conditions that are too difficult or too remote for large airplanes.

The ultramodern subway system in Caracas

The first railway was built in Venezuela in 1835, to connect the Aroa Mines in the Segovia highlands to Tucacas. Twenty years later construction began on a line between Caracas and La Guaira, but this was not completed until 1883. The line was slow and not economical and was closed by President Medina Angarita in the 1940s.

An almost total lack of interest in railway transport changed in 1976, when the government announced plans to build a 2,423-mile (3,900-kilometer) network at a cost of 10,000 million bolívars to be completed in 1990. A series of problems brought the work to a halt soon after it was begun. More successful is the new underground railway in Caracas. Inaugurated in 1983, with a basic network of 32 miles (52 kilometers) and 51 stations, it is air conditioned, comfortable, and quicker than any other form of city transportation.

Venezuela has nine major ports, thirty-four petroleum and mineral ports, and five fishing ports. Most important are La

Guiara, the port for Caracas, which handles mainly imports. Maracaibo is the principal port for the oil industry. Raw materials for the Valencia industrial district pass through Puerto Cabello, and Puerto Ordaz on the Orinoco deals with shipments of minerals. With the majority of exports and imports being moved by sea, it is important that ports are equipped well enough to avoid congestion. With this in mind, new docks have been built at La Guiara, and port facilities are being improved and expanded elsewhere.

COMMUNICATION

In the 1970s, television was dominated by imported programs, especially from the United States. In the 1980s, the government decreed that television and radio should play more Venezuelan music and produce more educational and cultural programs. This has been a successful change and now Venezuelan television films are being shown in other parts of South America. There are four television channels, two are private and two belong to the state. Between them they transmit to over 60 percent of the national territory.

In 1986 there were over 6,500,000 radio receivers and over 2,500,000 television receivers in use. The government operates Radio Nacional from Caracas and commercial stations exist in all state capitals and in the two federal territories.

Radio arrived in Venezuela in 1930, when businessman William Phelps saw an opportunity to advertise his electrical products and cars. As programs took shape, there was a strong element of local culture, folklore, and music, as well as soap operas. Inevitably radio came to be of use to politicians, whose message could be transmitted to the remote corners of the country. It also played, and still does, an important part in relaying programs of educational interest to rural schools.

There is freedom of the press in Venezuela and over forty newspapers are published daily. *La Religión*, a Catholic publication, was founded in 1889 and is the nation's oldest newspaper. From Caracas, *Meridiano* has a circulation of about 300,000 and *Ultimas Noticias*, 250,000. *El Nacional* and *El Universal* have good domestic and international news coverage. Important newspapers in Maracaibo are *Panorama* and *La Crítica*. Most provincial cities publish at least one daily paper. The *Daily Journal*, founded in 1945, is an independent English-language newspaper published in Caracas.

Among the many magazines, the oldest, *Elite*, dates back to 1925 and is of general interest. Other include *Venezuela Gráfica*, which is a weekly, illustrated newsmagazine, and *Páginas*, which is a woman's weekly. Other specialist magazines cover subjects such as finance, politics, and hobbies. Some business institutions publish lavish house magazines, such as *Topico* produced by the petrol company Maraven. Leading international news agencies such as UPI and Reuters have representatives in Caracas.

The telephone service is run by the national company CANTV. In 1981 national telephone subscribers passed the one million mark. Most major cities are now linked by direct dialing, and have telex facilities. DDI (Direct Dialing International) is also possible between Venezuela and most areas of the world.

A ROLE IN THE WORLD

As a producer and exporter of oil, Venezuela has a world role. It was a founding member in 1970 of the Organization of Petroleum Exporting Countries (OPEC).

Venezuela joined the Andean Pact in 1973, with Ecuador, Peru, Colombia, and Bolivia. The group's objective was to plan industrialization and a common policy of investment, but progress has been slow.

Venezuela is also a member of the Organization of American States (OAS), the Inter-American Bank (IAB), the Latin American Free Trade Association (LAFTA), and the Latin American Economic System (SELA) established in 1975 with the aim of creating multinational enterprises. As a member of the Contadora group, with Mexico, Colombia, and Panama, Venezuela is working to achieve a peaceful solution to Central American problems. Venezuela also belongs to the United Nations.

Oil has been largely responsible for the republic's relationship with the United States. Early in the twentieth century, investors were welcome and as revenues increased, North American culture and consumer goods were eagerly acquired. The North American way of life was easy to see: fast cars, drive-in movies, and hamburger bars. Some people resented the North American presence, but mostly it became a part of the Venezuelan life-style. When nationalization of oil occurred, Venezuela could afford adequate compensation for the North American companies and it was a reasonably amicable separation. Relations became strained with the United States, however, when Venezuela strongly supported Argentina in the Falklands (Las Malvinas) War.

Diplomatic missions from more than sixty countries are represented in Caracas.

When Venezuela's neighbor, British Guiana, gained independence and became Guyana, the border dispute between

A statue of Simón Bolívar in Caracas

the two countries continued. In 1970 it was agreed in the Port of Spain Protocol to put the matter aside for twelve years, but during the early 1980s, border skirmishes were again reported. Most recently the United Nations has been asked to mediate.

Venezuela also is in conflict with Colombia over maritime boundaries at the mouth of Lake Maracaibo, which have never been properly settled. Events took a serious turn in mid-1987 when an incident involving a Colombian warship put both countries on full military alert for a time.

In June 1983, Venezuela was host to several hundred Latin American politicians and intellectuals who met in Caracas to discuss the future prospects of Latin America and the Caribbean. The event was to commemorate Simón Bolívar's bicentenary, and the Bolívarian Declaration of Caracas at the end of the conference reaffirmed his old dream of continental unity.

The administration of President Lusinchi indicates that Venezuela would like to improve relations with its neighboring Caribbean islands. In past years Venezuela has contributed significantly to private and public investment in the region. Future foreign policy suggests that Venezuela may play a leading role in that area.

VENEZUELA'S FUTURE

Few countries can count themselves as fortunate as Venezuela. Rich in oil, natural gas, minerals, and with great potential for hydroelectric energy, the country has most of the resources necessary for a strong economy.

During this century Venezuelans have learned that they must not rely on income from a single product. Oil revenue has brought great wealth to the country, but a collapse in world prices has resulted in a troubled economy.

Governments have been quick to realize that they must diversify the economy. Industrial development of Ciudad Guayana and exploitation of Guiana's mineral resources must succeed. So too must efforts to increase agricultural production to make the country as self-sufficient as possible in foodstuffs. Venezuela has to address the problem of its foreign debt and how to make repayments to international and development banks. All the time the debt remains a problem, government spending and expansion will be affected.

More people now live in towns in Venezuela than they do in any other country in South America. This is creating a serious problem, as there are not enough jobs or good houses for people who come from rural areas looking for work. With a relatively

Black Lagoon in the Andes

small population, the trend to move from rural areas must be stemmed as people are needed for agricultural work.

Popularly elected democratic governments have now ruled Venezuela for thirty years. This in itself is a remarkable achievement, considering the early history of military and dictatorial rule that existed in the republic almost without interruption since independence. This transformation is partly due to the realization by political leaders that social reform is necessary to improve conditions, particularly for the poor in all regions of the country. Already a good start has been made and care has been taken not to upset the traditional representatives of wealth and authority. Political stability is as vital for progress as a strong economy is for future growth and prosperity. Venezuela can look forward to the twenty-first century with optimism.

MINI-FACTS AT A GLANCE

GENERAL INFORMATION

Official Name: Republic of Venezuela (República de Venezuela)

Capital: Caracas

Official Language: Spanish

Government: Venezuela is a federal republic. Its most recent constitution was written in 1961. It provides for a president, elected for a five-year term by direct universal suffrage; and a Congress, composed of a popularly elected Senate and a Chamber of Deputies. Former presidents may serve in the Senate. All legislators serve for five years. The president is ineligible for reelection for ten years.
Everyone over the age of eighteen is eligible to vote.

Flag: The flag has three horizontal bands—yellow, blue, and red, with a crest in a corner of the yellow band and a semicircle of seven stars in the middle of the blue band. The colors come from the banner flown by Simón Bolívar; the stars represent the seven provinces.

National Anthem: "Gloria al Brave Pueble" ("Glory to the Brave People")

Religion: Roman Catholicism is the traditional religion, though the constitution guarantees freedom of worship.

Money: The basic unit is the bolívar. Rates fluctuate widely. In 1987, one rate of 7.50 bolívars to the U.S. dollar applied to "priority" imports such as medicines and food, and another rate of 14.50 bolívars to the U.S. dollar applied to raw materials for industry.

Weights and Measures: Venezuela uses the metric system of weights and measures.

Population: Estimated 1988 population—20,116,000; 81 percent urban, 19 percent rural

Major Cities:

Caracas	1,261,116
Maracaibo	1,151,933
Valencia	889,228
Barquisimeto	681,961

(Population figures based on 1988 official estimates.)

GEOGRAPHY

Highest point: Pico Bolívar, 16,423 ft. (5,002 m)

Lowest point: Sea level along the coast

Mountains: The Andes range is the highest mountain system in the country. The Sierra Nevada is the highest and largest Andean range. The mountains paralleling the Caribbean contain most of the major population centers.

The Llanos, or plains, a region with an almost level relief, extend for about 800 mi. (1,287 km) to the Andean foothills. South of the Orinoco River and bordering Brazil and Colombia are the Guiana Highlands, a mountainous mass that is one of the largest granite blocks in the world.

Rivers: The 1,284-mi. (2,066-km) Orinoco River drains most of the Llanos and Guiana Highlands, emptying into the Atlantic Ocean through a number of tributaries, including the Apure and the Caroní rivers. It is one of the four major river systems on the continent of South America. There are more than 1,000 rivers in Venezuela.

Climate: Though variable according to elevation, the climate is generally tropical, with the seasons marked more by differences in rainfall than temperature. At Caracas, for example, the average annual temperature is 70° F. (21.1° C). Areas such as the northern coastal plains and the Caribbean islands are arid, whereas the windward mountain slopes are generally well watered. In over three-fourths of the country the wet season lasts from April to October or November.

Greatest Distances: North to South: 790 mi. (1,271 km)
East to West: 925 mi. (1,489 km)

Coastline: 1,750 mi. (2,816 km)

Area: 352,145 sq. mi. (912,050 km²)

NATURE

Trees: About one half of Venezuela is covered with forest of some kind. Most of the plant life of Venezuela is tropical and nondeciduous, retaining its foliage throughout the year.

The zones above 10,000 ft. (3,048 m) have a typical alpine landscape with bright yellow flowers called *frailejones* and lupins and gentians. Along the Caribbean coast the forest becomes increasingly dry and assumes the character of a thorn forest, with many cacti and thorny legumes.

In the south and east there is a large rain forest of tall trees and a dense canopy of branches and lianas and scant undergrowth.

The national tree is the araguaney.

Animals: Jaguar, puma, ocelot, wild dog, marten, otter, monkey, nutria, porcupine, tapir, and peccary are common. There are also deer and opossum. Crocodiles, alligators, and turtles are found along many streams. Boa constrictors and other snakes as well as lizards abound in the jungles.

Domestic animals include cattle, goats, sheep, and swine.

Birds: Herons, cranes, storks, ducks, and other waterfowl are numerous in the lowlands, and many large birds of prey occupy the highlands.

One of the most extraordinary birds is the *guacharo,* or oilbird, which lives in caves in forested places.

Migrants such as whistling ducks are often on their way north or south from the Caribbean and North America.

Fish: Despite the long coastline and many lakes, fishing is not an important part of Venezuelan industry. Sardines, shellfish, and tuna are caught in significant numbers, however.

EVERYDAY LIFE

Food: The basic item on the Venezuelan menu is the *arepa,* a flat corncake toasted on an earthen pan. Stuffed with chicken, pork, eggs, olives, and capers it becomes *hallaca,* a national dish that is served mainly at Christmas. A thick soup of vegetables and meat or chicken is called *sancocho, Hervido* is a soup with chunks of meat, chicken, or fish boiled with vegetables or roots.

Flat, maize pancakes called *cachapas* are cooked on an iron griddle and can be filled with savory mixtures or cheese and are often sold at the roadside.

Among the popular sweets is *huevos chimbos,* egg yolks boiled and bottled in sugar syrup.

Venezuelan beer, twice as high in alcohol as North American beer, is a popular drink

Housing: Housing is in short supply, and many Venezuelans live in squatter villages on the outskirts of the cities.

In the 1960s the government embarked on a massive program of public housing. Caracas became a modern city of high-rise apartment buildings in the 1960s.

Modern, functional blocks of apartments can be found in almost every part of Venezuela.

The most common residential dwelling is the *rancho*—simple brick shacks or, in their more affluent version, adobe dwellings often with tile roofs in colonial style.

Indians like the Yanomani live in individual "homes" under a large circular thatch shelter called a *yano.*

Holidays

New Year's Day, January 1
Carnival, Monday and Tuesday before Ash Wednesday

Holy Week, Thursday and Good Friday
Declaration of Independence, April 19
Labor Day, May 1
Independence Day, July 5
Bolívar's Birthday, July 24
Day of the Public Functionary, September 24
Columbus Day, October 12
Christmas Day, December 25

Culture: The culture of Venezuela is primarily Spanish and African. The fine arts are influenced by trends in the U.S., Brazil, and Mexico. The principal folk type is the *llanero*, or plainsman, who suggests the gaucho of Argentina or the cowboy of the U.S. The llanero's folklore, songs, dances, and legends are popular throughout the country.

Venezuelans themselves have made important contributions to the plastic arts. The most important artist of the 19th century was Martín Tovar y Tovar, whose most famous canvases picture the epic battles for independence. Arturo Michelena painted religious and secular subjects on a grand scale. Antonio Herrera Toro is another famous muralist. The best-known 20th-century artist is Tito Salas. Jesús Soto is an important producer of kinetic art.

The great man of 19th-century letters was the poet and philosopher Andrés Bello. Outstanding authors who have received international acclaim are the novelist Rómulo Gallegos, whose 1929 novel, *Doña Bárbara* expresses a cautious optimism for his country's future, and the novelist and essayist Arturo Uslar Pietri. The historical fiction of Francisco Herrera Luque has recently broken records.

Musical expression is important to Venezuelan life. Different regions have individual musical styles. The government has sponsored one of the leading symphony orchestras in Latin America since the 1920s. The Institute of Culture and Fine Arts (INCIBA) promotes the publication of books and arranges for their free distribution, as well as maintaining various museums, academies, and cultural centers.

There are many learned societies as well as specialized, university, and government libraries.

The museums in Caracas include the Fine Arts Museum, the Bolívar Museum, the Museum of Colonial Art, the Natural Science Museum, the Museum of Military History, and the Museo Talavera, which contains exhibits of pre-Columbian and colonial artifacts.

Sports and Recreation: Spectator sports are popular and include fútbol (soccer), baseball (the national game), and bull fighting. Horse racing has been a national sport throughout the 20th century.

Beaches are crowded and snorkeling and scuba diving are popular. Good to excellent fishing can be found several hours from Caracas. Jogging, mountain climbing, and hiking are popular, as are tennis and hunting. Softball, volleyball, and fútbol are played in vacant lots.

Communication: Caracas has four national TV networks. Old American feature films, dubbed in Spanish, are shown frequently. TV newscasts provide good coverage of international news. In the past decade the government has encouraged the production of Venezuelan educational and cultural programs. There are many radio stations that broadcast traditional Latin American and popular U.S. music.

There are seven daily newspapers; three are important sources of opinion: *El Nacional*, a liberal newspaper, *El Universal*, a moderate and business-oriented newspaper, and *El Diario de Caracas*, which serves an intelligent, influential readership. Most provincial cities publish at least one daily paper.

The telephone service is run by the national company CANTV.

Transportation: The highway system is good, but often poorly marked. All major routes and connecting roads are paved. Gas stations and garages can be found throughout Venezuela.

Foreign carriers on international flights arrive daily in Caracas. VIASA, the Venezuelan International Airline, has flights to U.S., as well as to other Latin American and European cities. Linea Aeropostal Venezolana is owned by the government and provides service to twenty-two airports in the least populated regions. Air taxis and helicopters fly to areas that are inaccessible to large airplanes.

Venezuela has only a few short stretches of railroad, mainly for freight, and a passenger line between Barquisimeto and Puerto Cabello. There is a new, efficient underground railway in Caracas. A national network of buses operates throughout the country.

Venezuela has nine major seaports, thirty-four petroleum and mineral ports, and five fishing ports.

Education: As in all the Spanish colonies, education during the colonial period was in the hands of the church and restricted to a very limited group. Schools were often attached to monasteries.

Today education in state schools, from the primary grades to the university, is free. Schooling is compulsory for all children between the ages of 7 and 15. Secondary education is less well developed, providing for only about 40 percent of the 13- to 17-year-old age group. Private schools play a significant role at both the primary and secondary levels.

Higher education is free to students who qualify. There are a number of public and private universities and teachers colleges and one polytechnic institute.

The literacy rate is at 85 percent and rising.

Health and Welfare: Health and welfare services are being expanded by the government. Sanitary facilities are being constructed; hospitals and rural medical centers are being built; and medical personnel are being trained. Medicine is both public (free) and private.

Health conditions are generally quite good. There is a low death rate and an increasing rate of longevity since World War II. Malaria, yellow fever, and other endemic diseases have been brought under increasing control.

ECONOMY AND INDUSTRY

Principal Products:
Agriculture: cotton, sugarcane, corn, coffee, rice
Manufacturing: refined petroleum products, petrochemicals, processed foods, textiles
Mining: petroleum, iron ore, diamonds, gold

IMPORTANT DATES

20,000 to 10,000 B.C. — People arrive in South America, almost certainly from Asia

2000 B.C. — Isolated tribes settle throughout region

A.D. 1498 — Columbus on his third voyage sights the South American mainland at a point in northeastern Venezuela

1499 — Alonso de Ojeda names the region Venezuela, or Little Venice

1509 — First European settlement in South America is established

1513 — Franciscan and Dominican missionaries found monasteries on the coast

1567 — Caracas is founded

1717 — Spain establishes the Viceroyalty of New Granada. (That viceroyalty, while based on what is now Colombia, also included what are now Venezuela and Panama, as well as the northern part of what is now Ecuador.)

1811 — Declaration of Independence from Spain

1815 — Spanish rule temporarily restored

1818 — Bolívar named president of the republic of Gran Colombia, the union of New Granada (Colombia) and Venezuela

1821 — The Spanish army is decisively beaten

1830 — Venezuela secedes from Gran Colombia and secures its independence

1846 — José Antonio Páez becomes the first president; remains the dominant political figure for almost twenty years

1846-70 — Civil wars between conservative and liberal factions disturb the peace

1870 — Antonio Guzmán Blanco attempts to stabilize the country

121

1892-99—General Joaquín Crespo tries to restore peace and order

1899-1908—Cipriano Castro rules Venezuela as dictator

1908-35—Juan Vicente Gómez rules Venezuela as dictator

1920s—Venezuela becomes world's leading exporter of oil

1935—General Eleázar López Contreras comes to power

1941—Venezuela breaks relations with Germany

1945—Revolution results in the presidency of Rómulo Betancourt

1946—National elections held

1947—Rómulo Gallegos, a committed reformer, elected

1951—Major Marcos Pérez Jiménez, another military dictator, comes to power

1953—Pérez Jiménez elected to a five-year term as president

1959—Pérez Jiménez overthrown; followed by democratically elected, left-of-center administrations; Betancourt reelected

1964—Dr. Raúl Leoni wins presidency in peaceful transfer of power

1968—Rafael Caldera elected president; continues programs aimed at improved social welfare and education

1983—Dr. Jaime Lusinchi becomes president, serves until 1989

1988—Carlos Andrés Pérez elected president

IMPORTANT PEOPLE

Armando Barrios (1920-   ), contemporary artist

Andrés Bello (1781-1865), scholar and author

Rómulo Betancourt (1908-81), politician, president from 1858-63; guiding spirit of the Acción Democrática

Simón Bolívar (1783-1830), soldier, statesman, and revolutionary leader; patriot, leader in fight for independence

Joseph Bonaparte (1768-1844), king of Spain, 1808-13

José Tomás Boves (1770-1814), royalist supporter

Luis Britto García (1940-   ), contemporary writer who mixes history and fiction

Manuel Cabre (1890-   ), twentieth-century painter

Teresa Carreño (1853-1917), famous pianist

Cipriano Castro (1858-1924), general and dictator, came to power in 1899

Román Chalbaud (1931-   ), theater and film director

Isaac Chocrón (1935-   ), theater and film director

Agustín Codazzi (1793-1859), postindependence writer; wrote atlas of natural resources

Christopher Columbus (1451-1506), first European to reach Venezuela, 1498

Joaquín Crespo (1845-98), soldier and political leader; seized power in 1892

Rómulo Gallegos (1884-1969), novelist, author of *Doña Bárbara,* 1929; first popularly elected civilian president of Venezuela, in 1948

Juan Vicente Gómez (1857?-1955), dictator, 1909-35; cruel and corrupt; ruled through apparatus of brutal police force; founded Institute of Fine Arts and Museum of Natural History

Padre José Gumilla (d. 1750), priest; writer of chronicles

Antonio Guzmán Blanco (1829-99), dominated politics from 1870-88; president and dictator

Guillermo Heiter (1915-   ), twentieth-century painter; emigrated from Czechoslovakia

Antonio Herrera Toro, nineteenth-century muralist

José Angel Lamas (1775-1814), composer

Juan Landaeta (c.1780-1812) composer of national anthem

Fernand Léger (1881-1955), artist of contemporary glass mosaics

Raúl Leoni (1906-   ), president from 1963-83; member of Acción Democrática

Eleázar López Contreras (1883-1973), became dictator, 1935; instituted liberal reforms

Jaime Lusinchi (1925-   ), president, 1983-89; attempted some reforms but reverted to dictatorial methods

Angel Luque, painter from Córdoba, Spain; emigrated to Venezuela in 1955

Isaías Medina Angarita (1897-1953), soldier, general, and statesman; president through most of World War II

Arturo Michelena (1873-93), muralist

Francisco de Miranda (1750-1816), first fighter for Venezuelan independence

José Monagas (1784-1868), conservative; twice president; freed slaves

Rafael Monasterios (1884-1961), landscape painter

Pascual Navarro (1923-   ), contemporary artist

Alonso de Ojeda (1465-1515), early explorer, reached South America in 1499

Alejandro Otero (1921-   ), famous contemporary artist

José Antonio Páez (1790-1873), leader in the fight against Spain; instrumental in breakup of Gran Colombia; established himself as dictator of Venezuela

Marcos Pérez Jiménez (1914-   ), military dictator from 1948-58; first senator
    of the Federal District, 1968

Carlos Andrés Pérez (1922-   ), president 1976, reelected in 1988

King Philip V of Spain (1683-1746), gave Caracas monopoly on trade with Spain,
    1728; created Caracas Company

Hector Poleo (1918-   ), painter

Pedro Ríos Reyna, first violinist and president of Venezuela Symphonic
    Orchestra

Simon Rodríguez (1771-1854), intellectual; tutor to Bolívar

Tito Salas (1889-   ), best-known twentieth-century artist

Otero Silva (1921-   ), early twentieth-century artist

Jesús Soto (1923-   ), famous contemporary artist; created sculpture in the
    Galería Nacional de las Artes

Fermín Toro (1807-65), postindependence political thinker

Martín Tovar y Tovar (1828-1902), muralist

Arturo Uslar Pietri (1906-   ), author

Amerigo Vespucci (1454-1512), explorer; America is named for him

Carlos Raúl Villaneuva (1900-   ), contemporary architect; designed
    University City

Alexander von Humboldt (1769-1859), scientist and naturalist; explored the
    Llanos in 1800

INDEX

Page numbers that appear in boldface type indicate illustrations

About the Author

Newly graduated with a degree in history from the University of Wales, Marion Morrison first traveled to South America in 1962 with a British volunteer program to work among Aymara Indians living near Lake Titicaca. In Bolivia she met her husband, British filmmaker and writer, Tony Morrison. In the last twenty-five years the Morrisons, who make their home in England, have visited almost every country of South and Central America, making television documentary films, photographing, and researching—sometimes accompanied by their children; Kimball, eighteen, and Rebecca, twelve.

Marion Morrison has written about South American countries for Macmillan's Lets Visit series, and for Wayland Publishers' Peoples, How They Lived and Life and Times series. This is Mrs. Morrison's second Enchantment of the World book for Childrens Press. Resulting from their travels, the Morrisons have created their South American Picture Library that contains more than seventy-five thousand pictures of the continent.